I0648229

Robert Lowth

A larger Confutation of Bishop Hare's System of Hebrew

Metre

In a letter to the Rev. Dr. Edwards: in answer to his Latin epistle

Robert Lowth

A larger Confutation of Bishop Hare's System of Hebrew Metre
In a letter to the Rev. Dr. Edwards: in answer to his Latin epistle

ISBN/EAN: 9783337318291

Printed in Europe, USA, Canada, Australia, Japan

Cover: Foto ©Lupo / pixelio.de

More available books at **www.hansebooks.com**

A LARGER

CONFUTATION

OF

BISHOP HARE's

SYSTEM of HEBREW METRE:

IN A LETTER TO

The Rev. Dr. EDWARDS;

IN ANSWER TO

His LATIN EPISTLE.

By ROBERT LOWTH, D.D.

F. R. SS. LOND. and GOETTING.

And Chaplain in Ordinary to HIS MAJESTY.

Αιψα κε φυλοπιδος πελεαι κορος ανθρωποισιν·
Ησιε πλειςην μεν καλαμην χθονι χαλκος εχευεν,
Αμηλος δ' ολιγιςος.   HOM.

LONDON:

Printed for A. MILLAR in the STRAND, and J. DODSLEY
in PALL-MALL.

MDCCLXVI.

A LETTER

TO

THE REV. DR. EDWARDS.

REVEREND SIR,

WHEN I firſt gave my opinion of the very learned and ingenious Biſhop Hare's Syſtem of Hebrew Metre[1], which my ſubject almoſt unavoidably led me to do; I ſupported that opinion with reaſons, which, as you yourſelf are pleaſed to acknowledge[2], merited ſome regard. In further ſupport of it, I afterwards added a *Confutation* of the ſame Syſtem, in a different form, and by a different argument; which I then thought, and do ſtill think, to be demonſtrative. Both theſe arguments were drawn from general principles; which, if true, left no ground for the Biſhop's Syſtem to ſtand upon. I did not trouble myſelf or my reader with a particular and ſcrupulous examination of all the ſeveral parts of the ſuperſtructure; which would have coſt much time and pains to very little purpoſe, and to the great diſguſt of both. I expreſly declined an under-

[1] De S. Poeſi Hebræorum, Præl. III.
[2] EDWARDS, Prolegomena in Libros V. T. Poeticos, p. 85.

A 2   taking

[4]

taking of this kind. I aimed at the very foundation of the whole building; and, I think, I overturned it from the bottom. In the Latin Epiftle, therefore, which you have done me the honour publicly to addrefs to me, I think you had no right to charge me with an artful diffimulation ³ in paffing over many of Your arguments in filence. I never undertook to anfwer, or to examine, all, or indeed any, of Your arguments. All that I attempted, and profeffed to do, was to fupport, againft One Objection of your's, what I had written before you ever publifhed a word upon the fubject: and even upon this head the whole of my argumentation was directed, as before, againft Bifhop Hare, and not againft You. As for the contradictions, which you have pointed out, between fome paffages of the lectures and the confutation; as likewife the falfe reprefentations, and difingenuous dealing, with which you have been pleafed to charge me; I fhall ftill keep the fame filence, though, now you have made the difcovery, it can no longer be called artful or cunning; nor will I offer any defence of myfelf in form. I fhall only refer to the feveral paffages ⁴ where you have pointed them out; that if any one thinks it worth

³ Epift. p. 3.
⁴ EDWARDS, Epiftola, p. 2, 3. 38, 39. (Compare his Prolegomena, p. 27.) Prolegomena, p. 95. 99. 231, 232.

while,

while, he may fee what grounds there are
for thefe accufations, and with what truth
and judgement they are laid before the public : and I fhall freely fubmit my caufe to
the verdict of common candor and common
fenfe.

As Profody and Metre is a fubject in itfelf exceedingly dry and unentertaining, and
efpecially Hebrew Metre, which, I am afraid,
is alfo very unedifying, and likely to recom-
penfe our trouble with little acquifition of
knowledge; I had fo much regard for my
readers, as to take care to give them as little caufe of difguft as poffible. I determined to fay only what I thought moft to the
purpofe; and to fay even that in as few
words as I could. The firft argument ⁵ I
endeavoured to exprefs with as much brevity,
as might be confiftent with clearnefs: the
Confutation I contrived to bring within the
compafs of four pages in *quarto*; and if it
had threatened to run to double the number,
I believe, for that very reafon I fhould not
have ventured upon it. But alas! with all
my care I have not been able to avoid, what
I fo much apprehended: you complain, and
you feveral times repeat your complaint,
ᵗ that I fatigue you, that I make you fick to
death. I flatter myfelf, that your ftomach

⁵ See De S. Poefi Hebr. Præl. III.
ᵗ Epift. p. 2. 33, 34. 41, 42.

A 3   muft

muſt be peculiarly delicate and faſtidious: for upon examination I find, that the whole that I have written upon this ſubjeɛt makes but ten pages in *octavo*. But whatever you may feel, does it become You to utter this complaint? I will not return the compliment in kind; but I have read, indeed I have! above three hundred pages of your's upon the ſame ſubjeɛt. Whenever I begin to exceed that number; you may then perhaps be allowed to complain, and cry out, *Ohe jam!* with ſome ſort of decency. But till then, I really think, that you are obliged in common juſtice to give me a patient hearing : eſpecially when I aſſure you, that what I now ſend you, was principally intended for your particular ſatisfaɛtion, by placing before you in a clearer light, if I could poſ-ſibly do it, ſome points that are in diſpute between us.

And here I muſt beg leave to abide by my former method; that of combating general and fundamental principles only, thoſe upon which the whole cauſe reſts, and, which removed, the whole muſt ſink. Were I to undertake to confute every auxiliary argument, and to anſwer every incidental objection, there would be no end of it : I ſhould much exceed the bounds above preſcribed; I ſhould never hold out myſelf; and what would become of You? It is merely for your relief and my own, that I proceed thus : not
out

out of an artful diffimulation, or with a
defign of declining the force of any argument, which I may pafs over in filence.
For fhould there be any fuch argument,
among all that have been hitherto publicly
advanced in fupport of this Syftem, either
by yourfelf or others, which, after having
confidered what I fhall here fay, you fhall
think of importance enough ftill to urge in
defence of it; I declare myfelf ready to anfwer it, and in fuch a manner, as I am perfuaded will be fatisfactory to every unpre-
judiced perfon.

I muft begin with a remark of your's which
occurs pretty far in your Epiftle; where you
tell me [7], that I have ftumbled at the very
threfhold, and am miftaken in faying, that
Bifhop Hare has deduced the laws of his Metre
from the CXIth Pfalm. Let us turn to his
book; let us fee how this matter ftands, and
carefully trace his method of inveftigation.
The Bifhop fets out with exhibiting this
Pfalm [8]: let him call it an example, or a
key, or whatever elfe he pleafes; that is not
material; let us fee what he *does* with it.
The periods of this Pfalm, the verfes, the
fyllables, are all determined; and the accents placed to mark out the metre. The
Pfalm thus ordered and adjufted, he immediately begins to reafon upon it; to make his

[7] Epift. p. 15.
[8] HARE, Prolegomena in Pfalmos, p. ii.

A 4 deduc-

deductions, and to draw his conclusions, in the form, manner, and words following : [9] " Hinc clare liquet :" " ex hoc Pſalmo " liquet :" " ex hoc Pſalmo conſtat : " " hinc certiſſime conſtat :" " ex hoc " Pſalmo clare conſtat :" " hinc ſequitur :" " ex verſibus ſexto & ultimo invicem " collatis liquet :" " in verſu quinto ex " metro liquet:" and ſo on. He [1] moreover *confirms* his obſervations on the CXIth Pſalm, by the CXIIth, CXIIIth, and CXIVth Pſalms; as they ſtand in his Book of Pſalms, divided and accented by himſelf in the ſame manner. He [2] then retraces, as he ſays, his own ſteps, and lays together in order the principal concluſions, which he had before drawn, all ariſing in the firſt place from the CXIth Pſalm ; for the three other Pſalms afford no new Canons of Metre ; they only confirm thoſe already drawn. Other concluſions indeed are deduced from them, concerning the reading, the pointing, and the pronunciation. But it is from the aforementioned concluſions, deduced from the CXIth Pſalm, and confirmed by the three following Pſalms, that he compiles his Canons or Syſtem of Metrical Laws, XI in

[9] HARE, Prolegomena in Pſalmos, p. iv. vi. vii. viii. xi. xii. xvii.
[1] Ibid. p. xviii.
[2] Ibid. p. xxvii.

num-

number [3]. In explaining the Bifhop's fcheme
you follow exactly the fame method, and ufe
the fame terms; only fomewhat hightened,
and for the moft part advanced to the fuper-
lative degree. Your account of the procefs is
this: the [4] beginnings and endings of the
feveral verfes in this Alphabetical Pfalm being certainly known, the learned Bifhop afterwards found, that thefe verfes were either
Trochaics or Iambics; (how he found this
out, and how it appears, that they are really
Trochaics or Iambicks, we fhall hereafter
confider:) and moreover other matters alfo
clearly appeared from this fame Pfalm, which
particulars you introduce in manner and form
following: " Ex hoc Pfalmo illud quoque
" liquido conftabat:" " ex hoc Pfalmo cla-
" riffime liquebat:" " ex hoc Pfalmo lucu-
" lentiffime patebat:" and this account of
the particulars you fum up in your four principal canons; which four contain very nearly
all of Bifhop Hare's. You introduce them
with thefe words: " En itaque quatuor præ-
" cipuos canones *ex hoc Pfalmo collectos*
" (Pfalmorumque univerforum auctoritate
" firmatos) quibus quafi fundamentis metrica

[3] HARE, Prolegomena in Pfalmos, p. xxvii, — xxxi.
[4] EDWARDS, Prolegom. Cap. II. See alfo his Preliminary Differtation to his Englifh Tranflation of the
Pfalms, p. 5,—8.

" Hariana

" Hariana nititur." 'This is evidently the form of the procefs, as it is laid before us both in the Bifhop's Prolegomena, and in Your's. The CXIth Pfalm is propofed, ready divided into periods and verfes, the verfes fcanned, the fyllables accented; you both reafon upon it, and draw conclufions from it, as from a matter perfectly well eftablifhed, and fettled beyond all doubt, in all its parts; and thefe conclufions you afterwards collect together into a body of Metrical Laws. And this was the very account that I gave of it: my words were thefe; "Proponitur [6] Pfalmus "CXI^{mus} in verficulos diftributus, et ac- "centibus notatus, unde deducendæ funt "leges Metricæ Hebrææ." Be pleafed to ob- ferve alfo, that I did not diffemble the Bi- fhop's plea, by which he claims the benefit of the confirmation, which his laws receive from the whole Book of Pfalms. I gave it

---

[5] So likewife in the Preliminary Differtation : " Thus, " from this CXIth Pfalm, Bifhop *Hare* difcovered the four " principal parts of his hypothefis." — " The truth and " certainty then of this hypothefis feems fufficiently to " appear from the abovementioned CXIth Pfalm." p. 8, 9. " What has been hitherto offered in favour of Bi- " fhop *Hare's* difcovery will, I hope, in fome meafure " fhew it to be rational and well grounded. But as this " has been entirely drawn from *one* of the Alphabetical " Pfalms, it may not be improper to lay before the read- " er fome of thofe, which are not Alphabetical ones, as " they will greatly *ftrengthen and confirm what has been al-* " *ready advanced*." p. 19.
[6] Metricæ Harianæ Brevis Confutatio, not. ult.

nearly

nearly in his own words, which are thefe:
" Hæc [7] autem quæ dixi vera effe, ut funt
" veriffima, conftat exemplis hic adductis;
" et cuivis Pfalmos infpicienti facile liquebit,
" cum quavis fere pagina exempla legenti
" in oculos incurrent." And I gave an anfwer to it; the propriety of which, I hope,
before I have done, fully to juftify.

Having cleared myfelf from the charge of
mifreprefentation, I proceed to inquire more
exactly into the Bifhop's method of reafoning; to trace his fteps clofely and warily; to
place his fyftem in a fuller light, than he has
been pleafed to afford to it; and to lay open
the whole foundations of it, which in his
Prolegomena feem to be rather withdrawn
from the reader's obfervation.

At the very entrance of the Prolegomena
the CXIth Pfalm is immediately exhibited to
our view, divided, fcanned, accented, all in
due form. By what authority all this is
done; and what proof there is, that it is
truly and rightly done, we are not yet informed. The proof certainly does not pre-
cede the Pfalm: we are to fuppofe, that it
will in due time follow, and be communi-
cated to us at laft: and in the mean while
we muft be content to take it upon truft,
that it is truly and rightly divided, fcanned,
and accented. The firft obfervation that the

[7] HARE, Prolegom. p. xxxi.

Bifhop

Bifhop makes upon the Pfalm is, " ' That
' it is an Alphabetical Pfalm, the feveral let-
' ters of the Alphabet, each letter in its order,
' beginning the feveral verfes; which marks
' the limits of the verfes, their beginnings
' and endings; fo that we cannot be mi-
' ftaken in dividing them, in making any of
' them longer or fhorter than they ought to
' be. The Pfalm therefore, as there given,
' is rightly divided into its verfes.' We rea-
dily admit it: the argument is unexceptiona-
ble. Again, ' The [9] word *Hallelujah*, as it
' ftands by itfelf, before the initial letter *Aleph*,
' with which the firft verfe begins, does not
' belong to the verfe.' Very right; the proof
is fatisfactory; we allow it. The author
proceeds: " In [1] this Pfalm the periods are
" in number ten; the firft eight of which
" are diftichs, the two laft are triplets:
" ―― for it is manifeft, both from the me-
" tre, as I fhall prefently fhew, and from
" the fenfe, that the two laft periods cannot
" be divided into three." There is nothing
in this conclufion, confidered in itfelf, that
appears improbable: on the contrary, the
fenfe, as it is here alledged, feems rather to
recommend it to our favour, and inclines us
to acquiefce in it.

[8] HARE, Prolegom. p. iii.
[9] Ibid. p. iv.
[1] Ibid. p. iv. v.

We

We have hitherto been led on fairly and openly: we have had all the satisfaction, which we could demand, in the two firſt inſtances; two undeniable proofs, of the right diviſion of the verſes, and of the excluſion of *Hallelujah* from making part of the firſt verſe. And ſomething probable is now offered from the ſenſe in favour of the diviſion of the two laſt periods; and further ſatisfaction is promiſed from the metre.

But here we muſt be upon our guard: at this very place the impoſition commences; and if we take a ſtep further without due caution, we may not eaſily be able to recover ourſelves. The truth of the diviſion of the two laſt periods is to be proved, it ſeems, from the metre. But the metre itſelf is not yet proved: it was laid down at firſt without proof: not a ſyllable has yet been advanced in proof of it: how then can any thing be proved from it? Should a mathematician in the courſe of a demonſtration refer, for proof of ſome ſtep in his reaſoning, to a theorem, which he had not yet demonſtrated; his demonſtration would turn out at laſt no demonſtration at all. But let us ſee, what this promiſed proof is, and in what manner it is given. We come to it in the next page [2]; and it is to this effect: " It is plain from this Pſalm, that it is not neceſſary, that all the periods of the ſame

[2] HARE, Prolegom. p. vi.

poem

poem fhould be of the fame kind of metre:
for here the firft, fixth, eighth, and tenth,
are plainly of one kind, but the reft of another. The former may not undefervedly be
called Trochaics; the reft Iambics. For in
the former the accent is to be placed on the
firft fyllable, that the verfe may have a right
cadence; but in the reft an acute accent is to
be placed on the fecond fyllable; as the reader will eafily perceive by the accents here
placed. From this Pfalm it is certain, that
the verfes of the fame period ought to be of
the fame kind; namely, in diftichs both the
verfes are either Trochaics or Iambics.—The
fame thing is obferved in periods confifting
of three members, as it is plain from the
two laft periods of this Pfalm, in both of
which all the verfes are of the fame kind.
— From [3] what has been faid it clearly
appears, that the two laft periods of this
Pfalm are rightly conftituted, and ought
not to be divided into three diftichs; for
the laft verfe of the ninth period is an
Iambic, and the firft of the tenth a Trochaic."

Every fingle propofition of this argument
is advanced without any authority whatever,
other than that of the Pfalm above-mention-
ed, as it is divided, fcanned, and accented,
at the editor's pleafure, and laid down with-

[3] HARE, Prolegom. p. vii.

out any proof at all of its being rightly done: and the whole, and every part of it, being deduced as a confequence from a mere arbitrary fuppofition, in no one part proved, except the divifion of the verfes, and the exclufion of *Hallelujah*, in many parts not even probable, cannot itfelf pretend to any higher degree of certainty.

It is indeed aftonifhing, that the learned author fhould think he would be quit of his promife at this rate. The thing which he promifed to prove was this: that the two laft periods of the CXIth Pfalm were rightly conftituted, in being divided into two triplets, and not into three diftichs. And how does he prove it? Even thus: The feveral verfes in the fame period *ought to be* of the fame kind; for they *are* fo in this Pfalm. In this Pfalm the two laft periods *are* rightly divided; for verfes of the fame period *ought to be* of the fame kind; which here they would not be, if the periods were divided otherwife. Each of thefe two propofitions; namely, verfes of the fame period *ought to be* of the fame kind; and, this Pfalm *is* rightly divided into periods; is in its turn affumed: and each of them in its turn, in the compafs of a fingle page, is urged as the proof, and deduced as the confequence, of the other.

The

The argumentation from hence forward
to the conftitution of the Canons ᵃ is wholly
of the fame kind (excepting only the VIth
fection ⁵, which confutes the hypothefis of
Le Clerc), all deduced from the CXIth Pfalm,
as adjufted in the very entrance of the Prolegomena; and from the CXIIth, CXIIIth,
and CXIVth Pfalms, as adjufted in like
manner at the editor's pleafure in the book
itfelf. Thefe three latter Pfalms, called in
to aid and fupport the former, do not make
the leaft alteration in the cafe. The proof,
that they are rightly divided, fcanned, and
accented, is ftill wanted. We do not complain of a deficiency of quantity in Pfalm
CXI, but of a deficiency of proof. If it were
four times as long, it would be juft the fame
thing: add yet another, and yet another Pfalm;
add the whole Book of Pfalms, even though
it contained fifteen hundred inftead of a
hundred and fifty, divided, fcanned, and accented, in like form and manner; we are
ftill but juft where we were, till it be demonftrated, that they are thus rightly divided, fcanned, and accented, according to
the genuine laws of metre, the quantity of
fyllables, and the true pronunciation and cadence of verfe, among the antient Hebrews.
Suppofe Gomarus, Meibomius, and Le Clerc,

⁴ HARE, Prolegom. p. xxvii.
⁵ Ibid. p. viii. ―― xi.

had

had purfued their feveral fchemes; and had divided, accented, fcanned, rhymed, the whole Book of Pfalms, as no doubt they could have done, according to the fpecimens which they have feverally given: would this have been a proof of the truth of each of their fyftems? or rather, would not this fingle proof of the truth of each have been a demonftration of the falfity of them all; of all at leaft but one?

But it may be imagined, that the author chofe to proceed in this method for the eafier explanation of his Syftem; and only intended, that we fhould give him credit awhile for the truth of his fcanfion, till he fhould give us the demonftration of it in a more convenient place. Now I beg to know, where he has done this: turn to the Prolegomena; find out the place, and be fo good as to point out to me the demonftration. I profefs I have fearched for it in vain. Having deduced and formed his Canons of Metre, in the manner already explained; as if his bufinefs were quite done, and his Syftem eftablifhed beyond all contradiction, the author now proceeds to give an account of the ill fuccefs of others in the like attempt and of the caufes of it; and then paffes on to other matters, not neceffarily connected with the prefent queftion, which he never refumes. In his notes he perpetually argues from his Metre in the fame manner, as a thing already perfectly eftablifhed. In fhort, the great *defideratum* is no where to be found : the verity of the fcanfion of the CXIth Pfalm is left juft as it ftood in the entrance of the Prolegomena; and fo likewife, the divifion, fcanfion, and accentuation of all the reft of the Pfalms in the Bifhop's edition, is left naked and defti- tute of demonftration, of all colour or fha- dow of proof whatfoever.

This is a begging of the queftion fo grofs and palpable, that, though I only give an account of a matter of fact, about which every one may be fatisfied by examining the Book itfelf, yet I am apprehenfive it may ad- mit of fome doubt merely from the improba- bility of the thing. How is it poffible, may it be afked, that a perfon fo ingenious, fo learned, and fo acute, as Bifhop Hare cer- tainly was, fhould fo impofe, 'either upon himfelf, or others ? I do not know how to account for it, but from the ftrength of pre- judice, which a fpecious Hypothefis carries along with it ; when it happens to ftrike the imagination, and by pleafing the fancy in- finuates itfelf into the approbation of the judgement. This once effected, it takes faft hold of a man's mind ; it poffeffes him in- tirely : he can neither hear, nor fee, nor un- derftand any thing that thwarts his Syftem ; and there is no camel of an abfurdity, which he cannot fwallow with eafe. This perhaps

might

might be fufficient to fatisfy other people, and to induce them to inform themfelves, whether the cafe be really, as I reprefent it, or not. But what fhall I fay to You, Sir; who, I perceive, are actually inclofed within the magic circle, and are under the very wand of this enchantrefs? It is a defperate attempt : however I will try, whether I cannot diffolve the charm, and fet you free. All I require is, that you would make fome effort to open your eyes, while I endeavour to place the thing before you in another light.

The whole Syftem of Bifhop Hare con-fifts of two diftinct parts : one is the diftri-bution of the Pfalms into periods and verfes, and the fcanfion and accenting of the verfes; this, to avoid the multiplying of words, I fhall call the New Metre : the other is, the fettling of the pronunciation of the Hebrew, and the correction of the Maforetic Pointing; this I fhall call the Reformed Punctuation. Thefe two parts, though diftinct in them-felves, yet have here a neceffary dependence upon one another : take away the New Me-tre, and the Reformed Punctuation, which is deduced from it, falls to the ground; take away the Reformed Punctuation, which in-troduces a different numeration of fyllables, and the New Metre cannot fubfift. If either of thefe parts were once firmly eftablifhed upon a folid foundation; the other, by its con

nex ..

nexion with it, might be in fome meafure
fupported. If the New Metre were delivered
to us upon fufficient authority, fuch as the
exprefs teftimony of one of the antient Prophets, as David, fuppofe, or Ifaiah, or Ma-
lachi; (for I cannot admit of any later teftimony upon this point:) or by a Divine Revelation, fuch as Meibomius pretended to
have received; (a pretence highly impudent
indeed and profane, but in other refpects not
injudicious, for by what other means could
he come by his knowledge?) a Revelation, I
mean, well and duly attefted: or if it were
clearly inveftigated by reafon and argument;
(any good argument not drawn from the Reformed Punctuation, for that is the thing
fought in this cafe, and as yet fuppofed to be
unknown:) the New Metre, I fay, being in
any of thefe ways antecedently proved, and
unqueftionably eftablifhed, the Reformed
Punctuation might then be fairly deduced
from it, in the manner in which we fee it
done in the Bifhop's Prolegomena. On the
other hand, if the Reformed Punctuation
either were indubitably proved by deduction
of reafon and argument, (fuppofing it capable of fuch proof;) any argument, I mean,
not drawn from the New Metre, for that is
in this cafe the thing fought, and hitherto
unknown: or were it confirmed by fufficient
authority, fuch as the exprefs teftimony of
one

one of the antient Prophets, raifed from the
dead, fuppofe, (as Samuel is thought to have
been by the Witch of Endor) and fpeaking to
us with an audible voice : or laftly, were it
delivered to us by Divine Revelation; the
only method indeed, by which, as far as I
can conceive, it is poffible for us to arrive at
the knowledge of it : the Reformed Punctuation being thus antecedently eftablifhed, fome
parts, though not the whole, of the New
Metre might from thence with fome fhew of
probability be deduced. But as the cafe now
ftands, as neither of thefe parts, feparately
and independently of the other, is eftablifhed
on any fuch proof; they are both of them
mere creatures of the imagination, abfolute
fictions, void of all folidity or reality whatfoever.

To come to particulars; let us examine the
form and manner of the Bifhop's reafoning
in an example or two, brought forward, and
fully difplayed in open light.

Pfalm CXI.   Verfe, or Line, 11th.

" Cóh maysáv higgíd leyámmo."

This verfe is marked and accented as a Trochaic. Why is it a Trochaic ? " Becauf:
" it confifts of an even number of fyllables."
How do you prove it to confift of an
even number of fyllables ? " Thus; c 6
                    B 3   " is

" is one fyllable; *maysav* is two fyllables;
" *higgid* is two; *leyammo* is three : in all eight
" fyllables." Or fhorter thus; " *maysav*"
(the only doubtful word, fuppofe, as to the
number of fyllables) " is a diffyllable; *there-*
" *fore* the 11th verfe is a Trochaic."

Now turn to Prolegomena, p. xvi. " It
" is plain from the 11th verfe, that *maysav*
" is a diffyllable." How fo? " Why *be-*
" *caufe* the verfe is a Trochaic." In other
words; " The 11th verfe is a Trochaic;
" *therefore maysav* is a diffyllable."

Again; Pfalm CXII. Verfe, or Line, 17.

pizzár náthán l'ebjónim.

This verfe ftands as an Iambic. How do
you prove it to be an Iambic? " *Becaufe* it
" confifts of an odd number of fyllables."
How do you make out the number of fyllables? " Thus; *pizzar* two fyllables; *nathan*
" two; *l'ebjonim* three; in all feven fyllables."
Or fhorter, thus; " *l'ebjonim*" (the only
doubtful word) " is a triffyllable; *therefore*
" the 17th verfe is an Iambic."

Now turn to Prolegomena, p. xix. " It
" is plain from the Metre, that *l'ebjonim* is
" to be read as a triffyllable." How fo?
" Why, *becaufe* the verfe is an Iambic."
That is, in another order of words; " The
" 17th verfe is an Iambic; *therefore l'ebjo-*
" *nim* is a triffyllable."

Thus

Thus the Reformed Punctuation proves the New Metre, and the New Metre proves the Reformed Punctuation: the caufe is the effect, and the effect is the caufe: a difputation in a circle, from which no valid conclufion can be drawn, except that of the futility of the hypothefis, which is built upon it.

The proof of the kind of verfe from the number of fyllables is never drawn out in full form, and unfolded, as I have done it in the examples above given : but the reafon is always implied ; and it arifes from the IVth and Vth Canons : which are themfelves affumed, as I fhall hereafter fhew, without the leaft proof, or even probability, whatever. But the proof of the number of fyllables from the kind of verfe lies open [6]. Hence if we take a general view of the Syftem, as it ftands in the Prolegomena, the apparent form of it is fuch, as I have before reprefented it: that is, the New Metre only feems to be taken for granted, and the Reformed Punctuation to be deduced from it. But in truth, both the one, and the other are, each in its turn, equally taken for granted, without proof; and the whole argument,, conclufion as well as premiffes, is altogether a mere begging of the queftion.

[6] See Prolegom. p. xii. xvi. xvii. xviii. xix, &c.

Having

Having ſhewn, that the truth of Biſhop Hare's Syſtem of Hebrew Metre is not proved; I ſhall now proceed one ſtep further, and ſhew, that it is in itſelf falſe and abſurd, and utterly incapable of proof.

The Four [7] firſt Canons or Laws of Hebrew Metre, as the author has given them, are the Four Corner Stones of the whole Edifice. I ſhall try the ſtrength of them; if they give way, the whole building falls to the ground. The reſt, were the Syſtem true, are of very little importance.

I. " In this Poetry all the feet are diſſyl-" lables."

II. " No regard is had to the quantity of " ſyllables:" or, " There [8] is no difference " of long and ſhort ſyllables."

The former of theſe propoſitions is deduced as a conſequence of the latter [9] : I ſhall take them both together into conſideration.

The Biſhop in his Prolegomena is very brief upon theſe two material articles, and affords us but very little light upon the ſub-

[7] Note, that by the Four firſt Canons I mean Can. I. II. IV. and V. The III[d] is an inſignificant propoſition, which ſeems to have been numbered as one of the Canons in the Prolegomena, p. xxvii. by miſtake.
[8] Prolegom. p. xii.
[9] Ibid.

ject.

ject. The whole that he says amounts to
this : " It ' clearly appears from this Pfalm,
" that in the Hebrew Poetry no regard is
" had to the quantity of fyllables. — Hence
" it follows, that all the feet in the Hebrew
" Poetry are diffyllables." I fhould have
thought the confequence much more obvious
and juft, if he had faid : " Hence it follows,
" that in the Hebrew Poetry there are no
" feet at all." However he is going to clear
up this matter ; he fubjoins a reafon for it ;
a medium, by which he proves the confequence. " For, fays he, if there were any
" feet confifting of three fyllables, the dif-
" ference of fhort and long with regard to
" the middle fyllable would neceffarily take
" place in this, as well as in the Greek and
" Latin Poetry." The argument in form muft
ftand thus :

In all Poetry every triffyllable foot has the
middle fyllable of a determinate quantity ;
(that is, either long or fhort :)

But in the Hebrew Poetry there is no determinate quantity of fyllables :

Therefore in the Hebrew Poetry there are
no triffyllable feet.

I beg leave to borrow this curious argument ; and to carry it one ftep further, where
we fhall find it to be equally conclufive.

' Prolegom. p. xi. xii.

In

In all Languages every word of three fyllables has the middle fyllable of a determinate quantity [2]; (that is, pronounced either
long or fhort:)

But in the Hebrew Language there is no
determinate quantity of fyllables :

Therefore in the Hebrew Language there
are no words of three fyllables.

So much for the Bifhop's argumentation.
You, Sir, are pleafed to be more large on this
head. You begin with it in your Epiftle to
me. I had intimated, that I fuppofed there
was a manifeft contradiction in Metre, in
Iambic and Trochaic Feet and Verfes, without difference of long and fhort fyllables. I
thought, that a hint was fufficient; and that
there was no neceffity of explaining at large,
that as the very nature and effence of an
Iambic Foot confifted in its being made up
of two fyllables, the firft fhort, and the fecond long; and of a Trochaic Foot, the reverfe, the firft long, and the fecond fhort;
therefore, where there was no difference of
long and fhort fyllables, there could be no
Iambic and Trochaic Feet; and where there
were no Iambic and Trochaic Feet, there

---

[2] Common fyllables are very few in any language;
but they belong properly to Poetry only, and are indeed
a Poetic Licence. " Nam verfuum *propria* conditio eft ;
" *ideoque* in *his* quædam etiam [fyllabæ] *communes*."
QUINTIL. ix. 4.

could be no Iambic and Trochaic Verſes : and
that to talk of Metre without long and ſhort
ſyllables, was like talking of an army without men, a fleet without ſhips, and a grove
without trees.   However You ſeem not to be
apprehenſive of any difficulty in this affair ;
and tell me, that [2] if I do not underſtand,
what Metre is without difference of long and
ſhort ſyllables, I muſt acknowledge, that I
know nothing of Engliſh Metre.   This I
cannot quite allow : as an Engliſhman, one
of the many, who has read a good deal of
Engliſh Poetry, and has a tolerably good ear,
I muſt aſſert my right of giving my judgement on this ſubject; and therefore ſhall
preſume to examine what You have ſaid
upon it.

You acknowledge, that [4] we have verſes,
which exactly anſwer to certain Metres of
the Greeks and Latins; but yet, that this
difference of long and ſhort ſyllables is not
obſerved, nor can be obſerved, in our language, whoſe nature is ſuch, that it cannot
admit of it. This, you ſay, every one knows,
and that it is too manifeſt to be denied. You
are too apt to follow your Author's example,
in taking for granted what ought to be proved.
What you affirm, concerning the nature of

[2] Epiſt. p. 4.
[4] Ibid. p. 5.

our

our language, is fo far from being felf-evi-
dent, that every one, who knows any thing
of the matter, cannot but know the contrary
to be true.

Let us confider your very firft example of
Englifh Verfe.

" He fúng and héll confented ;
" Stern Próferpíne relénted."

You fay, thefe are very like, and exactly anfwer, to the Anacreontic Metres : as,

Θἔλῶ λἔγεῖν Α'τρεῖδας,
Θἔλῶ δἔ Κᾱδμὄν ᾳδειν.

And why, I beg to know, are they not as
properly and abfolutely Iambic Verfes as thofe
of Anacreon? Why is not *hĕ fŭng* as truly
and properly an Iambic Foot as Θἔλῶ? *and
bĕll,* as λἔγειν? You very ⁵ properly diftinguifh
between the Rules by which the quantity of fyllables in Greek and Latin, and thofe by which
the *accent* (you could not confiftently with
your Hypothefis fay, the *quantity*) in Englifh,
is determined : and yet you will perhaps tell
me, that though *and* is long by pofition, ne-
verthelefs it here obtains the place due to a
fhort fyllable ; and fo of the reft : for this is
the Bifhop's language, and you follow it by
faying, that fuch fyllables *may be accounted*

⁵ Epift. p. 6.

fhort,

fhort, and others *may in a certain manner be taken for long*; as if they were not really fo. Now I fay, that *and*, as a particle without emphafis, is naturally fhort; and the fame is to be faid of the pronoun *he*: that the firft in *confénted* is fhort, and more determinately fo than the firft in Ἀτρείδας; this may be long, but that cannot: that *ftern* is long, as the firft fyllable is in the line of Anacreon next to thofe you have quoted: that the middle fyllable in *Proferpine* is neceffarily fhort according to the Englifh pronunciation; though the fame fyllable in *Proferpina* according to the Latin form, and even in *Proferpine* [*] according to the Latin pronunciation, be neceffarily long: that Pofition in Englifh does not always, nor even generally make a fyllable long; that even in Greek and Latin it is far from being a general rule; that in Greek there is a multitude of exceptions from it [7]; and for the Latin I refer you to Hare De Metris Comicis, p. LIX, &c. I will not be

[*] See Milton, Parad. Loft, Book IV. 269.
[7] See Dr. Clarke's Note to Homer's Iliad. II. 537. To the examples there given add ὄγχνη, Odyff. xxiv. 246. ἀνδρότης, Iliad. XVI. 857. συγγάμβρος, Euripid. Phœnif. 431. ἀμπλακήματα, Æfchyl. Eumenid. 937. in all which a vowel is made fhort even before Three Confonants. The Critics indeed in moft of thefe places raife doubts concerning the genuinenefs of the reading, rather from the difficulty arifing in regard to the quantity, than from any other valid reafon.

anfwer-

anfwerable for his being right in all his examples: but I need not trouble myfelf about
that; *ipfe dixit*; and I dare fay, You will not
queftion his authority. I might add, that [a] in
Greek and Latin there are degrees of long
and fhort fyllables; that there are fyllables
ftill longer than long fyllables, and ftill fhorter
than fhort fyllables; and therefore, that neither all long fyllables, nor all fhort fyllables,
are equal to one another in quantity; fo far
is quantity even in thefe languages from being of an abfolutely determinate nature: and
laftly, that in Englifh perhaps there is no
certain limit fixt by nature to determine,
what degree of pofition is fufficient to make
a fyllable abfolutely and neceffarily long in
verfe.

In the fame manner you [b] compare fome Englifh Verfes with fome antient Trochaics; and
fay, that one might not without reafon affirm
of the former, that they confift of Trochaic
Feet, and that they ought to be ranked in
the number of Trochaic Metres. You feem
to argue with me, as if I denied it: on the
contrary, I affirm more pofitively, than You
dare to do, that they are really Trochaic
Verfes, and confift of real Trochaic Feet, as
much as thofe of Anacreon. And as to Your

[a] DIONYS. HALICARN. De Structura Orat. Sect. XV.
QUINTIL. IX. 4.
[b] Epift. p. 8.—10.

Hebrew

Hebrew Verfes, which you produce, I am
fo far from denying them to be Trochaics and
Iambics, fuppofing the pronunciation to be
rightly noted, and the accents rightly placed,
that I infift upon it, that they are really Trochaics and Iambics; and moreover that they
confift of real Trochaic and Iambic feet;
otherwife they could not be, nor rea-
fonably be called, Trochaics and Iambics.
Whenever you talk of this matter, you
fpeak, after the example of your author, with
great referve and caution: your Verfes are
non immerito to be accounted Trochaics and
Iambics; and your fyllables may *quodammodo
be taken for* long or fhort. Like the fub-
ftance of Epicurus's Gods ', " non eft cor-
" pus, fed *quaſi* corpus; non fanguis, fed
" *tanquam* fanguis:" they are not Trochaics, but *as it were* Trochaics; nor Iambics,
but *as one may fo fay* Iambics. " Mirabile
" videtur, quod non riferit Epicureus, cum
" Epicureum videret: hoc mirabilius, quod
" vos inter vos rifum tenere poffitis." There
is fomething at the bottom of this management: I fancy, I fhall difcover the whole
fecret by and by. But whatever your defign
may be, your reafoning wholly depends, on
this fuppofition, that ' the modern Lan-

' Cicero De Nat. Deor. Lib. I. 26.
' " Omnium hodiernarum linguarum, quatenus de
" fyllabarum quantitate agitur, eadem eft ratio quæ

guages, Englifh, French, Spanifh, Italian,
&c. admit not a difference of long and fhort
fyllables ; that therefore the Hebrew may
have been of the fame nature in this refpect.
At prefent therefore I fhall purfue this fubject
a little further.

Now, Sir, as You have very well obferved,
and proved it by twenty quotations, that the
ear is the fole judge of numbers or metrical
founds ; and as You have fo good an ear, as
to be able to judge perfectly well of the
found of Hebrew Verfes, not one fingle verfe
of which language, rightly pronounced, you
have ever yet heard, or can poffibly ever hear :
what can I do better than appeal to your ear ?
Your ear muft furely be a ftill better judge of
Englifh Verfe : this you can rightly exprefs,
and commit to your ear, by your own voice.
For " though the ear" (fays Longinus [3] as
you quote him) " be the judge, the voice
" muft fet it in order : for as the voice ex-
" tending and contracting the found of the
" well-modulated rythme formeth the fylla-

" Hebraicæ: nempe ita comparatæ funt, ut brevium.et
" longarum difcrimen—refpuant atque repudient." ED-
WARDS, Prolegom. p. 134. " Ex hoc Pfalmo clare con-
" ftat, nullam in Poefi Hebr. quantitatis fyllabarum ra-
" tionem haberi :—quod et hodie obtinet in omnibus, ni
" fallor, Europæis linguis." HARE, Prolegom. p. xi.
[3] In Fragmentis.

" bles,

" bles, fo the ear receiveth it from thence,
" and judgeth of it." Now Longinus in
this cafe would certainly have required the
voice of a Native, and not of a Barbarian :
and if you had attended to the fenfe of this
fecond quotation of yours, you would have
feen, that all the reft of your quotations were
nothing to the purpofe, and that this quotation totally overturned all that you had been
endeavouring to eftablifh.

I beg you then to try the feveral examples,
which you have produced, by your Voice and
Ear ; and to tell me, whether you do not find,
that Pope's, or Dryden's, or Milton's, Trochaics or Iambics, run as well, and ftrike the
ear, as to cadence, number, and accent, as
fully and diftinctly, as thofe of Anacreon ? You
fay yourfelf, that the Correfpondent Verfes
are exactly * alike, and perfectly fellows or
twins : whence then proceeds this exact likenefs, which by your own account amounts as
near to an identity, as poffible ? I fhould
think, from the likenefs, or rather the fame-
nefs, of the caufe : namely, that the Englifh
Trochaic and Iambic Verfes confift of Trochaic and Iambic Feet, juft as much as the
Greek do. But how can that poffibly be, if
in Englifh there be no difference of long
and fhort fyllables ?

* Epift. p. 11.

C   I beg

I beg you to try likewife fome examples of another kind.

" 'Tis [5] her crime to be lov'd ;
" 'Tis her crime to have charms.
" Let us fly ; let us fly :
" She fhall die ; fhe fhall die :
" In my rage fhall be feen
" The revenge of a Queen."

Can you find among the Greek Tragedians any Anapæftic Verfes, that ftrike the ear more diftinctly and forcibly, than thefe ? I fay among the Greeks ; for among the La-tins, (whofe language, for an obvious rea-fon [6], is not fo well fuited to thefe numbers) I believe, you will fearch in vain. I will give you one example more in the fame kind.:

' See,' wild|as the winds,|to the de|fert he flies !"

which, if you pleafe, you may refolve into Dactyls (for where there are Anapæfts, there muft be Dactyls ; as where there are Iambics, there muft be Trochees) thus :

---

[5] ADDISON's Rofamond.
[6] " Quia [apud Latinos] ultima fyllaba nec acuta un-
" quam excitatur, nec flexa circumducitur ; fed in gravem,
" vel duas graves, cadit femper." QUINCTIL. xii. 10.
[7] POPE's Ode on St. Cecilia.

" See,|wild as the|winds to the|defert he|flies!"

At leaft, the following are Dactyls; or, as perhaps you would have me fay, and, as you cannot but own, fomething exceedingly like Dactyls indeed, and which may not undefervedly be called fo:

" Merrily, [8] merrily, fhall I live now,
" Under the bloffom that hangs on the bough."

And now, Sir, I muft afk you, why you would deal fo unfairly by us, as [9] to impofe upon us the authority of Dr. Bentley in a cafe, in which you would not fubmit to it yourfelf? For in the very fame page, in which Dr. Bentley had faid [1], that the Englifh Language admits not of dactylic meafures, (which you thought much to your purpofe, as it might feem to imply, that it admits not of triffyllable feet) he gives two examples which are directly contrary to the point which you would eftablifh. For to fupport the pofition of no quantity in Englifh Metre, you are driven to the neceffity of affirming, that [2] there are no triffyllable feet in Englifh Verfe. Now would you have us fubmit to the authority of

[8] SHAKESPEAR's Tempeft.
[9] EDWARDS, Prolegom. p. 97.
[1] De Metricis Terentianis, p. x.
[2] Epift. p. 34, 35.

C 2   Dr.

Dr. Bentley at the middle of the page, while you yourself reject the same authority lying directly before you at the bottom of the same page; where he gives examples of trisyllable feet, namely, Bacchiac and Cretic Feet, in English Verse? And pray, what need of having recourse to authority at all in this case? Cannot we read English, and have not we ears, as well as Dr. Bentley? Or, would you maintain, that there are no Anapæsts nor Dactyls in English, because|Dr. Bentley says so; and believe him rather than your own senses?

In short, the state of the case, as it stands now in dispute between us, is, I think, this: my ear affirms positively, that in English there are real Trochees and Iambics, and also real feet of three syllables, even Anapæsts and Dactyls, whatever Dr. Bentley may say: and your ear, I believe, will allow, that there is something very exactly corresponding to them, and very like them.

But supposing there should be in English quantity of syllables, yet there remain many modern languages, by the example of which you may still maintain your position of no quantity in the Hebrew; as French, Italian, &c. As to this matter, I cannot trust either your judgment, or my own: though our ear may receive verses in those languages rightly modulated, and exactly delivered to it, by the voice of a Native; yet there is something very delicate in this affair, of which we must

not

not pretend to be perfect judges. This is one of thofe cafes, in which it is proper, and even neceffary, to have recourfe to authority: and it is not the authority of every Native, that will fatisfy me in this point. It muft be the authority of one perfectly well acquainted with his own language : a perfon of tafte, of learning, and well verfed in the polite world. Let us confider the French Language ; and if we can find any fuch perfon to inform us of the nature of it in this refpect, let us abide by his decifion. I believe you will allow the Abbé D'Olivet of the French Academy to be fuch a perfon; one whofe authority in this cafe is unqueftionable. He has written a Treatife on this very fubject, intituled, De la Profodie Françoife. I fhall only give you in fhort his decifion, which is clear and full to the purpofe. He makes Quantity one of the chief heads of his difcourfe, and gives a definition of it : " Troifièmement, on met plus ou " moins de tems à prononcer chaque fyllabe, " en forte que les unes font cenfées longues, " et les autres brèves : et c'eft ce qu'on ap- " pelle *Quantité*." And he concludes his chapter on quantity thus : " On verra claire- " ment par-là, que nous pourrions nous faire " des régles de quantité auffi fûres, et réduites " à un auffi petit nombre, que celles du Grec " et du Latin." Indeed Monfieur D'Olivet gives it as his opinion, juft after the defini-

tion

tion above quoted, that quantity is effential to every language : and I am perfuaded, that you may as well endeavour to find out a language without vowels and confonants, as without long and fhort fyllables.

Perhaps you may allow, that in thefe modern languages there is indeed a fort of quantity, fomething that may not undefervedly be called a difference of long and fhort fyllables : but that it is not fo determinate, fo conftant and regular, as in Greek and Latin ; that the fame monofyllable is ufed fometimes as long, and fometimes as fhort ; and in words of many fyllables, the fyllables not accented are often dubious. But are the accents undeterminate, and the accented fyllables dubious ? For nothing lefs than this will at all ferve your purpofe. You muft introduce a total anarchy in accent as well as quantity, before you can in the leaft countenance your Hebrew Metre. Is it not *Jávoh*, and *Javóh*; *bécol*, and *becól*; indifferently in almoft every Pfalm of the Bifhop's fcanning ? Do we not fee *lévolám*, and *levólam*; *jéfarim*, and *jefárim*; *yedóthecá*, and *yédothéca*: *yábdecá*, and *yabdíca*, and fo of many other words, with like variation, occurring perpetually, and even in the fame Pfalm ; for inftance, the CXIXth Pfalm ? Is this too juftified by the example of the Englifh poetry, or by that of any language that ever exifted ? I urged this to you; and you ³

³ Epift. p. 31.

quote

quote upon me fome verfes of Milton, by
way of anfwer. Are your Hebrew Trochees
and Iambics then as determinate as Milton's
Englifh ones ? Or does Milton vary the accent
and quantity of the fame word perpetually,
as Bifhop Hare does? If after thefe lines,
which you quote,

    " Thén to cóme in fpíte of fórrow,
    " And át my window bíd good-mórrow,".

Milton in the next page of his poem, had
come with *forrów* and *góod-morrów*, would
not you have thrown Milton and his poem out
of the *windów* ?

In fhort, you fet out with a pofition ab-
furd in itfelf, and true in no fenfe at all;
that there is no difference of long and fhort
fyllables in the modern languages: you amufe
us with this for fome time by a vague and
loofe manner of talking about it. But when
we come to apply this pofition to your practice, it will not, even in your own fenfe of
it, in the leaft ferve your purpofe. An in-
difcriminate licenfe of altering in verfe both
the accent and the quantity of words from
their ufual and eftablifhed place and value in
common difcourfe, was never allowed in any
poetry of any language in the world.

So much for the two firft Canons; no
triffyllable feet, and no difference of long

    and

and fhort fyllables, in Hebrew poetry. I proceed to the two next; and fhall take them
likewife both at the fame time into confideration ; for thefe too are intimately connected,
and muft ftand or fall together.

⁴ IV. " When the number of fyllables is
" even, the Verfes of that kind may not un-
" defervedly be taken for Trochaics, to be
" pronounced with an acute accent on the
" firft fyllable."

V. " If the number of fyllables be odd,
" they are to be efteemed Iambics, and the
" fecond fyllable, that the rythme may be
" be preferved, is to be made acute."

Now, Sir, I am forry to do it, but I muft
beg you to fupport yourfelf as well as you
can, while I *repeat* what I faid before upon
this matter : only a few lines, I give you my
word. I afked, ' Whence is it certain, that,
" when the number of fyllables is even, the
" verfe is a Trochaic ; when odd, an Iambic ?
" Does it neceffarily arife from the nature of
" the Trochaic and Iambic Verfe ? By no
" means ; (for in the Trochaic and Iambic
" verfes of the Greeks and Latins rather the
" contrary holds) but from the mere will and
" decree of the author. Why therefore may
" not I, or any one elfe, in this CXIth Pfalm,
" or in any others whatever, place the accents

----

⁴ HARE, Prolegom. p. xxvii.
⁵ Metricæ Harianæ Brevis Confut. not. ult.

" in

" in a manner directly contrary, and turn
" *Hare's* Trochaics into Iambics, and his
" Iambics into Trochaics?" By [6] your anfwer
to me, you feem not to underftand this. I
endeavoured to exprefs my fenfe as fhortly, as
poffibly I could, to avoid giving difguft : this
perhaps has led me into obfcurity. I will now
dilate it a little, and explain myfelf fo fully,
that you fhall not fail to comprehend my
meaning.

Bifhop Hare's Rule is this : count the number of fyllables of which your verfe confifts ;
if the number be even, (fix, eight, or ten,
fuppofe,) the Verfe is a Trochaic ; if uneven,
(five, feven, or nine, for example,) it is an
Iambic. Now I afk, why not juft the contrary ? why is not the Verfe confifting of an
even number of fyllables an Iambic ; and that
of an uneven, a Trochaic ? If the Bifhop's
Rule is a good one, and founded in reafon, he
has left us to find out the reafon, as we may ;
for he has not given the leaft hint of it. I
was cafting about for it ; and confidering,
whether there was any thing in the nature
of Trochaic and Iambic Verfes, that determined one to an even, and the other to an
uneven, number of fyllables. And as for the
nature of thefe Verfes, how can one better
inveftigate it, than by examining it as it
appears in the writings of the Greek and

[6] Epift. p. 27—31.

Latin

Latin Poets, which give us the beft and
moft perfect examples of the feveral kinds
of them? Now I obferved, that the practice
of the Greek and Latin Poets, into which
they were certainly led by the genius and
nature of thefe Verfes, was rather contrary
to the Bifhop's rule; their Trochaics oftener
than otherwife confifting of an odd number
of fyllables, and their Iambics of an even number. And I beg you to obferve, how tenderly
and modeftly I expreffed myfelf upon this
occafion: for in truth the cafe is thus, for
much the greater part of all the Trochaics
and Iambics of the Greek and Latin Poets
that are extant. The Iambics and Trochaics,
moft commonly ufed by them beyond com-
parifon, are the Trimeter Iambic, and the
Trochaic Tetrameter Catalectic [7]: the former of which confifts of an even number of
fyllables, and the latter of an odd number;
the irregular feet in each, as Tribrachs,
Dactyls, Anapæfts, being reckoned as two

[7] " Verfus, quo *maxime gaudet* [Terentius] in Trochaico
" genere, quique jucundiffime et fumma cum venuftate
" decurrit, una fyllaba ab hoc deficit, inde dictus Tetra-
" meter Catalecticus: Latini Septenarium dixere." HARE,
De Metris Comicis, p. xlix. " Accedo ab Iambicum
" Trimetrum, quem Latini Senarium dixere; verfum lon-
" ge nobiliffimum, et *omnium maxime* a fcenicis poetis
" *frequentatum.*" Ibid. With regard to the Trochaic Tetrameter Catalectic, it is remarkable, that all the *extempore*
verfes of the Roman foldiers and of the mob, of which
Suetonius gives many examples, are of that kind.

fyllables,

syllables, as they represent dissyllable feet; otherwise it is to no purpose to talk at all of determining the even or odd number of syllables belonging to either. Or, to put this in another light, both Trimeter Iambics, and Tetrameter Catalectic Trochaics, end with an Iambic foot; which determines every regular Verse of the former kind to an even number of syllables, and every regular Verse of the latter kind to an odd number. And to what can it be ascribed, that Verses of both these kinds end in this manner, but to the harmony, the rythme, the cadence, that is, to the nature and genius, of these kinds of Verse?

The case is the same even in English. The Verses of the Iambic kind, most commonly used, and most universally prevailing, in our Poetry, are those consisting of four or five Iambics with single rhymes; and these have an even number of syllables. Of the Trochaic kind, the Dimeter Catalectic, of an odd number of syllables, is frequently used alone; the Dimeter Acatalectic, of an even number, is hardly ever used, without being alternately interchanged, or frequently, but irregularly, mixed with the other.

To make all this the more evident, I shall subjoin examples of the several kinds of Verse above mentioned, in Greek, Latin, and English.

I A M-

I A M B I C S.

TRIMETER :

Ω τεκνα, Καδμȣ τȣ παλαι νεα τροφη,
Τιναϛ ποθ᾽ εδραϛ ταϛδε μοι θοαζε|ε
Ικ]ηριοιϛ κλαδοισιν εξεϛεμμενοι ;

" Phafelus ille, quem videtis, hofpites,
" Ait fuiſſe navium celerrimus."

" Such was the fov'reign doom, and fuch the
    " will of Jove."

TRIMETER BRACHYCATALECTIC :

" The wrath of Peleus' fon, the direful
        " fpring,
" Of all the Grecian woes, O Goddefs,
    " fing."

DIMETER :

" But come, thou Goddefs fair and free,
" In heav'n yclep'd Euphrofyne."

All the foregoing are of an even number of
Syllables.

T R O C H A I C S.

TETRAMETER CATALECTIC :

Ω πα]ραϛ Θηϛηϛ ενοικοι, λευϛετ᾽, Οιδιπȣϛ οδε,
Οϛ τα κλειν᾽ αινιιματ᾽ ηδει, και κρα]ιϛ@ ην ανηρ,
Ειϛ οϛον κλυδωνα δεινηϛ συμφοραϛ εληλυθεν.
                                    " Cras

" Cras amet qui nunqu' amavit; quiqu'
" amavit cras amet.
" Ver novum, ver jam canorum; vere natus
" orbis eſt."

" Lovely ſeems the moon's fair luſtre to
" the loſt benighted ſwain,
" When all ſilvery bright ſhe riſes, gilding
" mountain, grove, and plain :
" But a thouſand times more lovely to her
" longing lover's ſight,
" Steals half-ſeen the beauteous maiden
" thro' the glimmerings of the night."

PERCY.

This ſeems to be the genuine form of the
Engliſh Trochaic, in one line of ſeven Trochees and a long ſyllable. But now this kind
of Trochaic in Engliſh is commonly divided
into two lines, or verſes; which diviſion was
probably occaſioned by the introduction of
the rhyme in the middle :

" Bred in plains, or born in vallies,
" Who would bid thoſe ſcenes adieu ?
" Stranger to the arts of malice,
" Who would ever courts purſue ?

" Malice never taught to treaſure,
" Cenſure never taught to bear,
" Love is all the ſhepherd's pleaſure,
" Love is all the damſel's care."

SHENSTONE.

And

And the Greek and Latin Trochaics of this
fort may be difpofed juft in the fame manner;
for they generally have the Cæfura at the
end of the fourth foot :

Ω πατρας Θηςης ενοικοι,
Λευσετ᾽, Οιδιπ8ς ὁδε.

" Cras amat, qui nunqu' amavit;
" Quiqu' amavit, cras amet."

By this divifion of the long Englifh Trochaic
into two Verfes, we have two forts of Trochaic commonly ufed : one the Dimeter Acatalectic, confifting of four Trochees, making
even fyllables ; the other the Dimeter Catalectic confifting of three, and a long fyllable,
making uneven fyllables.   This latter is frequently ufed alone in Poems of fome length;
of which many elegant examples may be feen
in Mr. Merrick's excellent Tranflation of the
Pfalms.   But the other is hardly ever ufed
alone; and for this obvious reafon : becaufe
the unvaried monotony of the cadence, if continued, would be extremely difgufting.   And
for the very fame reafon, Trochaics confifting
of an even number of fyllables were but little
ufed by the Greeks and Latins.

It appears then upon inquiry into this
matter, and on examination of Iambic and
Trochaic verfes, as practifed by the Greek,
Latin, and Englifh Poets, that, in refpect of
the number of fyllables, as even or odd, of
which

which they confift, the Iambic verfe is by its
nature, genius, and cadence, much more inclined to confift of an even number of fyllables, and the Trochaic on the contrary of
an odd number of fyllables, than otherwife.
So that if Bifhop Hare in forming his fcheme
of metre, had confulted the nature and genius of the Verfes, of which he made his
Hebrew Poetry to confift, and had been guid-
ed by them; he would have made both thefe
Canons directly the reverfe of what they are :
his verfes of an even number of fyllables would
have been, for the moft part at leaft, Iambics;
and his verfes of an odd number of fyllables,
would have been, for the moft part at leaft,
Trochaics. And then then thefe two Canons
would have been founded upon fome fort of
probability.

You fee, therefore, that it was not without
fome reafon that I afked, why I might
not be allowed to turn Bifhop Hare's Iambics
into Trochaics, and his Trochaics into Iambics ? which indeed, in my fictitious fyftem *
of Hebrew metre, I had actually done in feveral inftances in the CXIth Pfalm ; as,

> Odéh javóh becól lebáb,
> befód jefárim veyedáh.
> gédolím mayafé javóh.

* See Metricæ Harianæ Brevis confutatio.

4   And

And you now fee, that I had fome fort of reafon for doing fo, from the nature of the Iambic and Trochaic Verfe. And further, I had authority for doing fo from the Maforetic pointing, accenting, and pronunciation; which (excepting *jahvoh*, which is quite out of the queftion) are not altered by me in the above lines, but in one word only : whereas they are altered by Bifhop Hare in every word but one. Moreover, the prepofition *be*, occurring in each verfe of the firft diftich, being, by [9] your own acknowledgment, really and truly fhort, nay very fhort ; this circumftance alone determines that diftich to be, as I have marked it, Iambic.

But perhaps, Sir, you may fay, that I go upon quite a wrong principle in my pretended inveftigation of this matter : that the Bifhop proceeded upon much better and furer grounds: he did not attempt to deduce his Canons of Iambic and Trochaic Verfe from the nature of thofe verfes, as it appears from the Greek, Latin, and Englifh Poetry; or from the genius of thofe meafures in themfelves, always arbitrary and precarious, and varying with the differ-

[9] Preliminary Differtation, p. 15. Prolegom. in Libb. Poeticos, p. 27. " Fatendum fine dubio eft, (neque enim " verum diffimulabo) hafce fyllabas [*be* & *ve*] femper " breves fuiffe." And yet in his Epiftle, p. 39. he fays, that Bifhop Hare denies this very thing ; and this he proves by a quotation from Bifhop Hare ; which quotation indeed is nothing to the purpofe, for which it is brought.

ent

ent genius of nations and languages : he went
a' furer way to work ; he examined all the
Pfalms; and found experimentally, that the
fact was really fo ; that the verfes of an even
number of fyllables were Trochaic ; and thofe
of an odd number Iambic.

Now, Sir, I do take upon me to deny the
certainty of this pretended matter of fact.
Suppofe I fhould affirm, that I have examined
all the Pfalms ; and that I have found the
matter to be for the moft part quite otherwife ; that the verfes of even fyllables are
oftener than otherwife Iambics ; and thofe of
odd, Trochaics : admitting, what is by no
means certain, that the Hebrew Pfalms do indeed confift of Trochaic and Iambic Verfes ;
who fhall fettle this difpute between us ? what
is Bifhop Hare's authority in this cafe ? I
I will be bold to fay, not one jot better than
mine : for furely I may prefume to fee full as
well as the moft fharp-fighted man that ever
lived, when we are both alike in the fame
circumftances of abfolute and inextricable
darknefs. It is a cafe, that cannot be refolved
by any mortal upon earth : nor can I devife
any method of getting it properly decided,
but that, which I before propofed ; namely,
having recourfe to fome Witch of Endor, who
may affift us by raifing from the dead one of
the antient Prophets.

By this time, I hope, I have fully explained to you my meaning in the fhort queftion

D   or

or two, which I afked, concerning the two Canons of which we are treating: and you muft excufe me, if I have been too large and diffufe in my explanation; for, as they ftood before, I am fure you did not in the leaft comprehend what I meant, by your giving me anfwers fo very crofs to the purpofe. One of my queftions was, How is it certain, that, when the number of fyllables is even, the verfe is Trochaic; when odd, Iambic? You anfwer ' this by afking me, Whence is it certain, that this verfe, for example, is a Trochaic?

" Wóods and gróves are óf thy dréffing." I anfwer, Not at all, as you would intimate, becaufe it confifts of an even number of fyllables; for take away one of the fyllables, it will ftill be a Trochaic;

" Wóods and gróves are óf thy dréfs :" but becaufe, beginning from the firft, it is accented on the odd fyllables : and fo of your example of the Iambic. Do not you fee, that the verfes confifting of an even or odd number of fyllables, and their being accented on the even or odd fyllables, which laft is the only thing that determines them to be Trochaic or Iambic, are two things intirely diftinct and different, and that have no kind of connection or relation to one another? I afk again, Does this (that is, the Trochaic's con-

' Epift. p. 28.

fifting

fifting of even fyllables, and the Iambic of odd) neceffarily arife from the nature of the Trochaic and Iambic Verfe? Yes, you fay [2], it does : For Trochaic Verfes are to be accented on the odd fyllables, and Iambic on the even. The very fame anfwer in effect, and juft as wholly befide the purpofe, as the foregoing.

I fhall fay no more of Bifhop Hare's Four principal Canons : but after what I have faid of them, I fhall now venture to fet them down, and to fubjoin to them the Four principal Canons, which I oppofed to them in my fictitious fyftem.

I. " In the Hebrew Poetry the feet are all
" diffyllables.

II. " There is no regard had to the quan-
" tity of fyllables.

III. " When the Number of fyllables in
" a verfe is even, the verfe is Trochaic.

IV. " When the number of fyllables in a
" verfe is odd, the verfe is Iambic."

From what I have faid it appears, that every one of thefe propofitions is not only deftitute of proof, but even falfe, or in a great degree improbable.

My Four principal Canons are thefe.

I. " In the Hebrew Poetry the Feet are
" not all diffyllables.

II. " Regard is always had to the quantity
" of fyllables.

[2] Ibid.

III.

III. " When the number of fyllables in a
" verfe is even, the verfe is oftener than other-
" wife Iambic.

IV. " When the number of fyllables in
" a verfe is odd, the verfe is oftener than,
" otherwife Trochaic."

I only fuppofed, that thefe Propofitions were
equally clear and certain with the correfpond-
ing or oppofite Propofitions of Bifhop Hare;
and even on this fuppofition his fyftem was
demonftrated to be falfe. But from what I
have now faid, I believe, it appears, that thefe
Propofitions are in a good degree probable:
and therefore that my fictitious fyftem, though
on the whole deftitute of all proper foundation, in no one refpect fufficiently proved,
and in fome refpects certainly falfe, is never-
thelefs greatly preferable to that of Bifhop
Hare.

And here, Sir, I think, I might very well
let this matter reft, and leave the Harian
Metre from henceforth to maintain its ground,
and to keep itfelf upon its feet, fuch as it
hath, as it may. But as you fay, I have dif-
fembled fome of your ftrongeft arguments,
I fhall proceed a little further with you; and
as far as I can guefs what thefe weighty arguments are, I fhall take them into confideration. But I muft beg to be excufed from car-
rying my remarks upon them as far as I might
do; which perhaps would lead me into fome
very

very minute and tedious difquifitions. I fhall content myfelf with juft pointing out their weak parts; but in fuch a manner, as that any one converfant in thefe matters may be able to purfue them much further.

The argument, which you have urged, in favour of Bifhop Hare's Metre, from the genius of the Hebrew Language, feems to be a favourite one with you : for you repeat it, and infift much upon it. I had urged, and, as you are pleafed to allow, with fome pro- bability, that [3] as the Hebrew Language had now lain for above two thoufand years ab- folutely dumb and deftitute of its vowels, we cannot define with certainty either the num- ber or the quantity of the fyllables; and as thefe are unknown, the Metre, which intirely depends on thefe, muft be unknown alfo. You anfwer this by faying, that [4], though the Hebrew Language be deftitute of its vowels, yet the number of fyllables may in doubtful words be certainly defined; and as for the quantity, your metre has nothing to do with it. But let us hear the argument, as you have drawn it up in form : it is a Sorites; and be- hold, here it comes !

" The [5] *indoles* of the Hebrew Poetry be-
" ing known, the true number of fyllables

---

[3] De S. Poefi Hebr. Præl. III.
[4] EDWARDS, Preliminary Differtation, p. 14, 18, 19.
[5] EDWARDS, Prolegom. in Libb. Poetic. p. 85, 86.
Epift. p. 33.

D 3

" in

" in a very great number of words (*in quam*
" *plurimis vocibus*) will be known alfo:

" And of what kind the *ratio* of the He-
" brew Poetry is, you may certainly collect
" from the *ingenium* of the Hebrew Lan-
" guage:

" And of what fort is the *ingenium* of
" the Hebrew Language, is fufficiently ap-
" parent from hence, that Metrical Verfes
" cannot be written in it:

" And that Metrical Verfes cannot be
" written in it, is fufficiently clear from the
" multitude of long fyllables, and the paucity
" of fhort ones ; that is, from the frequency
" of the confonants, as Le Clerc has demon-
" ftrated in his Diſſertation on the Hebrew
" Poetry."

You further confirm this in your Prolegomena [6] by the teſtimony of Iſaac Voſſius ;
who obſerves, ' that the greater number of
' vowels there is in any language, the more
' perfect it is to be eſteemed ; and the fewer,
' the more rude it will be, and the more un-
' fit for Metrical Verfes.'

Now I beg leave to aſk, how you came to
be fo well informed as to your firſt principle,
from which you deduce all this curious reaſoning ? how did you inveſtigate and find out
the proportion, which the number of Vowels
bore to that of the Confonants in the Hebrew

* Ibid.

living

living Language? You set out with acknow-
ledging, that the Vowels have been lost a-
bove these two thousand years ; you do not
receive the doctrine of the Masorites as in-
fallible; no more did Le Clerc : by what rule
therefore do you make this computation? But
Bishop Hare has corrected and reformed the
Masoretical doctrine of the Vowel points.
Does he pretend then to have restored to us
the genuine Hebrew Vowels, and to have
given us the true antient pronunciation of
Hebrew, as far as it depends on the Vowels?
If he does, are we to take his word, and believe implicitly, that he has rightly and infal-
libly performed, what every man of common
sense must know to be absolutely impossible
for any mortal to perform? Nay, what Bishop
Hare himself has often in effect confessed to
be now impossible [7], and even to have been
impossible for the Masorites to have performed
many centuries ago; though much better
qualified, than he, or any one now can be,
to do it, by the traditionary pronunciation
delivered down to them in a continued suc-
cession from their ancestors? But Bishop
Hare himself does not pretend to so much :
he expresses his doubts with regard to the

[7] See HARE, Prolegom. p. xliv. l. li. " Nec profecto
" in ulla lingua vera pronuntiandi ratio certò sciri potest,
" nisi ab iis qui viva voce loquentes audierint eos, qui-
" bus lingua, de qua agitur, fuerit vernacula." HARE
de metris comicis, p. liv.

number

number of vowels, and the number of fyllables, in many forts and clafles of words,
which comprehend a confiderable part of the
language; and in particular with regard to
two cafes [b] ; which being left indeterminate
and free to be ufed either way, as he does in
reality leave them, he confefies it would be
fo enormous a licence, that the art of Hebrew
Verfification, very eafy otherwife, would be
rendered ftill fo much more eafy, as to become no art at all.

I am afhamed to fpend fo many words to
prove to you, what you muft be confcious of
yourfelf: namely, that you do not know,
what the true proportion was of the vowels
to the Confonants in the genuine pronunciation of the Hebrew Language; nor even
what it was nearly. You do not certainly
know, but that fome of the letters, (three or
four of them) which we now take for Confonants, were really Vowels. There are great
authorities [c] for this opinion; which, I believe, has never been effectually and altogether difproved. I will venture to add, that
you do not certainly know, but that the proportion of the Vowels to the Confonants might
be as great in the Hebrew, as it is in the
Latin, and even in the Greek. You may

[b] See HARE, Hebr. Pfal. Addenda, p. 1—4. & Prolegom. p. xlvii, xlviii.
[c] ORIGEN, JEROM, CAPPELLUS, WALTON, SIMON,
&c.

perhaps

perhaps think yourfelf fure in your nega-
tive here; but I fhall exhibit to you an experiment, which may poffibly ftagger your
faith.

The trueft idea, which we can now get of
the antient pronuntiation of Hebrew, is in
all probability to be had from the remains of
Origen's Hexapla. He has given us the expreffion of it in Greek Letters, according to
the pronunciation that obtained in his time.
His authority in this cafe is greatly fuperior to
that of the Maforetes, as he lived (according
the opinion almoft univerfally prevailing among
the learned) many centuries before the Maforetes had completed their fcheme of Punctuation : and the examples, which are preferved
in thofe remains, are much more ample and
fatisfactory, than what we find in the Septua-
gint, where we have only the like expreffion
of proper names. Here follow the three firft
verfes of Genefis, expreffed by Origen in
Greek Letters.

1. Βρησιθ βαρα ελωειμ εθ ασαμαιμ ουεθ ααρες.
2. Ουααρες αιεθα θωου ουβοου, Ουωσεχ αλ φνε θεωμ,
ουρουη ελωειμ μαραεφεθ αλ φνε αμαιμ. 3. Ουιωμερ
ελωειμ, ιει ωρ, ουιει ωρ.

Now in this piece of Hebrew, taken the
firft that offered, according to Origen, the
Vowels are to the Confonants almoft double
in number, eighty-one to forty-five. I will
let this argument reft here, till you fhall
produce an intire paffage, of equal length,
                                        taken

taken at pleafure, from any Greek author, profe or verfe, in which the number of the Vowels fhall bear to that of the Confonants a greater proportion.

Another argument in fupport of the Harian Metre, and a favourite one too, I fuppofe, for it is frequently and confidently urged; arifes from the evidence and teftimony of antient Verfions, and of parallel places; the coincidence of the fenfe with the Metre, and the great light thrown upon difficult paffages by the help of the Metre : all which confirm and prove the truth of the Bifhop's Hypothefis. Let us ftate this argument fairly, and fee what it amounts to.

Bifhop Hare has made a great number of alterations, and emendations, as they are called, in the Hebrew Text of the Pfalms : fome upon the authority of the antient Verfions and parallel places, others merely conjectural, fuggefted by the fenfe, the grammar, the context, and fome by the Metre alone. Now the whole of this evidence muft be laid together, before we can form a proper judgment upon it, and proceed to a well-grounded conclufion. If the antient Verfions, the parallel places, the context, the grammatical conftruction, fome or more of them, fometimes give evidence in favour of the rectified Metre, the fame witneffes, in conjunction with the Hebrew Text, at other times depofe

pofe directly againft it. It is very unreafon-
able to expect, that we fhould be fo partial
to the metrical Hypothefis, as to confider
only the favourable, and wholly to difregard
the unfavourable part of the evidence. The
fair and right way of proceeding is certainly
to take both into confideration ; to weigh all
circumftances; to balance one part againft
another ; and to fee the refult of the whole.
To fet this matter in a clear light, I fhall
give a plain example of this procefs upon one
of Bifhop Hare's Pfalms ; taking the firft of
them, that affords a fufficient number of
emendations ; but in no other refpect, that I
know of, more proper for my purpofe, than
any other whatever ; and that fhall be Pfalm
II. From this Pfalm I fhall produce all the
alterations that are made, in which the new
Metre is concerned, fee whether the above
witneffes depofe for or againft it, and fairly
fum up the evidence.

Period 2. line 1. *vai*jitjazzebu : *vai* added
for the fake of the Metre. The Hebrew Text,
and the antient Verfions, depofe againft this
addition. The Editor fays, the fenfe requires
it : this witnefs, being crofs examined, fays
no fuch thing. The evidence againft the
Metre.

Ibid. l. 3. *jah* for *jahvoh :* no other evidence in this cafe, but the Hebrew Text ;
and this againft the Metre.

P. 3. l. 1. *et* ſtruck out, for the ſake of the Metre. The Hebrew Text againſt this omiſſion : no other evidence appears. Againſt the Metre.

P. 8. l. 2. *haggoim*: *hag* added for the ſake of the Metre. The Hebrew Text, and antient verſions, againſt the addition : in particular the Greek Verſion, which has εθνη without the article; though the Greek idiom much inclined to admit it, and would certainly have done ſo, had the tranſlators found it in their copies. Here the Editor ſummons in favour of the addition a parallel place, Pſ. cxxxv. 12. (I ſuppoſe, it ſhould be 15.) This witneſs upon examination has nothing to ſay to the point. Againſt the Metre.

P. 11. l. 1. *jah* for *jahvoh*, as before. Againſt the Metre.

P. 12. l. 2. *Midderec*: *mid* added for the ſake of the Metre. Greek and Latin Verſion, and the Conſtruction, for the addition. I add likewiſe the Syriac Verſion. The evidence of the Hebrew Text ſet aſide in this caſe. Evidence for the Metre.

Ibid. l. 4. *veaſhre* : *ve* added for the ſake of the Metre. Hebrew Text, and antient verſions, againſt the addition. The ſenſe, called in in favour of the addition, hath nothing to depoſe. Againſt the Metre.

In Pſalm II. the emendations having been examined, the evidence againſt the new Metre,

I   ariſing

arifing from thence, is to that for the new Metre, as fix to one.

Now if you think, that upon examining the whole book of Pfalms in this manner, the evidence of this kind will turn out in favour of the new Metre, contrary to what it has done in this one Pfalm, you may try it, and let us know the refult of your inquiry: if you think otherwife, or fhould find it upon trial even more unfavourable, you had better drop this argument, and never urge it again for the future.

I muft obferve here, that the Harian Metre depending intirely upon the even or odd number of fyllables in each verfe, it is but an even chance whether any given alteration, which the fenfe, the conftruction, the parallel places, or the antient Verfions, may fuggeft, coincide with the Metre, or not; and though there fhould be no foundation at all for the Hypothefis, thefe teftimonies may be expected to appear as often in favour of the Metre, as againft it. But confidering the licences allowed of in the Harian, Metre, and the various ways of extending or contracting words, and making them of more or fewer fyllables, and even of dividing the fame word between different verfes; the chances are much in favour of the Metre, and it is great odds, but any given reading may with a little management be accommodated to it, and any given emendation be fet off fo as to feem to countenance it, it. This will moreover fufficiently account for the coincidence of the Hebrew Text of the Pfalms with the Bifhop's fcheme, fo far as it has fucceeded, helped out with fuch a number of alterations as he has ad-mitted. And it is very fairly to be prefumed, that with the fame licences, and the fame liberty of alteration, any part of the Hebrew Bible may be accommodated and adjufted to the faid Metre.

This objection has often been made; and 'it has been affirmed by thofe who have tried it, that the experiment has been attended with fuccefs. It has been anfwered on the other hand ', and that on experiment too, by a flat denial of the poffibility of the thing. What remains in this cafe, but to put the thing to the trial, and to exhibit the experi-ment; which no one yet on either fide has thought it proper, or worth while, to do. But firft with regard to two conditions, which are infifted upon as neceffary in this procefs; namely ', that the period be aptly divided, and the fentence be ended with the

' See EDWARDS, Prolegomena, p. 112.
' " Aufim affirmare, (quod etiam expertus loquor) " plane αδυναίον effe, falvis principiis, quibus *Harii* me-" trica nititur, ullum ex profaicis veteris teftamenti libris, " (immo vel unicam periodum, aut comma) nedum ullum " alium librum alia quavis lingua confcriptum, in ver-" ficulos metrice dividere." Ibid.
' ' Ibid, p. 113.

Verfe;

Verfe; it is to be obferved, that if thefe conditions are neceffary, there is at once an end
of Bifhop Hare's Scheme: at this rate perhaps half of his Trochaics and Iambics muft
be thrown out of his Pfalter. The truth of
the matter is; the moft apparent and general
Characteriftic of the Hebrew Poetry is its
being laid out into fentences nearly equal,
and in fome fort parallel; fo that the limits
of the Verfes for the moft. part probably co-
incided with the paufes of the fentences.
This is plainly feen in the Book of Job, and
in the Proverbs, and in many of the Pfalms.
But it is not univerfal : there are many others
of the Pfalms, which are in the whole, or
in part, very irregular in this refpect: thefe
cannot be reduced to Harian Metre upon
the above mentioned conditions: Bifhop
Hare himfelf could not do it. The conditions therefore are not neceffary upon his
principles *: and it will be fully fufficient
for the fupport of the above objection, and
the fuccefs of the experiment, if any given
part of the Hebrew Bible, confeffedly profe,
can be reduced to fuch Harian Metre, as
may be juftified by examples from the Harian

---

* " Manifeftum eft —— Singulos verfus fingulos fenfus
" non exponere. Quamvis plerumque verum fit, fingulos
" verfus colon, vel faltem comma integrum conficere,
" multis tamen exemplis liquet hoc non perpetuum effe,
" nec fane ex rei natura effe potuit." HARE, Prolegom.
p. xxxi. See alfo, p. xxi, xxii.

Pfalms;

Pfalms; to verfes as well turned, as well
divided, as regular, as elegant, as thofe of
Hare generally are; with no more licences,
or alterations of the Text, in adjufting them,
than are ufually admitted by the Bifhop
himfelf. And this I think any one may
venture to undertake. The firft trial I ever
made of this kind was upon the paffage that
firft came to hand; and without any difficulty it turned out as follows.

GENESIS I. 1 —— 5.

1. Béreſit bará elóhim
E't haſſámem v'ét haárez.

2. V'haárez hájetáh tohú vebóhu,
Véhoſéc yal péne téhom:
Verúh elóhim mérahépet
yál pené hamáim.

3. Vájomér elóhim;
Jéhi ór, vihí or.

4. Vájar élohím et háor,
C'i tob; vájabdél elóhim
Bén haór ubén hahóſec.

5. Vajíkra élohím laór jom,
Veláhoſéc kará lel:
Vihí yeréb, vihí bokér, jom éhad.

NOTE.

In this whole paffage there is but one
Letter altered. Period 5. line 2. for לילה
lailah,

lailah, I read לֵיל *lel*. God, in giving a Name to the Darknefs, it is prefumed, would be repre-fented by Mofes in this place, as making ufe of the proper and original form of that Name, not the improper and irregular; *lel*, and not *lailah:* for in the latter, when ufed as a noun, being ftill mafculine, the ה is paragogical, as the Grammarians inform us: fee *Buxtorf's Lexicon, Schultens Inftit. Ling. Heb.* p. 452. Befides, *lailah* is properly an adverb, (*Cocceii Lexicon*) *by night*, as *jomam by day*; (Deut. i. 33,) which latter alfo is ufed fometimes as a noun together with *lailah :* fee Jer. xxxiii. 20, and 25. For the fame reafon therefore that *jomam* is not ufed, nor could properly be ufed, in the preceding line, it is to be pre-fumed, that *lailah* could not be ufed in this. Reafon and Grammar require this emenda-tion, and the Metre confirms it. Note alfo, that לֵיל may be ufed in verfe, either way; indifferently [s], as a Monofyllable, or a Diffyl-lable.

The paffage above given affords but little matter for conjectural criticifm : and indeed the cafe is the fame throughout the whole chapter; in which the Text is in the main pretty intire, and free from miftakes of im-portance. I fhall therefore proceed no further here ; but pafs on to another place, the firft likewife, which naturally offering itfelf, with_

---

[s] See EDWARDS, note on Pf. lii. 8.

E   cut

out any particular fearch, feemed likely to
afford us larger fcope, and to give us an op-
portunity of difplaying our criticifm. We
fhall here fhew, that our Hypothefis, of the
Harian Metre univerfally prevailing through
all parts of the Hebrew Bible, greatly con-
duces to the emendation of the Hebrew
Text; and at the fame time the emendation
of the text will effectually recommend and
eftablifh our Hypothefis. But this, as a
matter of no fmall importance, we fhall
enter upon with due folemnity; and fhall
endeavour to execute in proper form, manner,
ftyle, and language, to the perfect fatisfaction
of the learned.

EXODI

EXODI CAPUT I.

I N

VERSICULOS METRICE divifum;

E T

METRICES præcipue OPE

Integritati fuæ reftitutum.

.

EXODI

CAPUT I.

1. " véclléh ſemót bené iſráel,
hábaím miẓráimah :
ét jaуkób *abíhem*
íľ ubéto báu.

5. reubén, ſimуón, leví, jehúdah ;
iſáſcar, zébulún, binjámin ;
dan, vénaptáli ; gád, veáſer :
vejóseр hájah bémiẓráim.

3. Hujuſce Libri Metrico-Hiſtorici (quod genus ſcriptionis an-
tiquiſſimis temporibus fuiſſe uſurpatum teſtantur auctores gra-
viſſimi ; quum non modo annales, ſed & leges metro conditæ,
rudium hominum memoriæ commendarentur:) hujus, inquam,
voluminis primum comma in codice Hebræo eſt tricolon, duobus
verſiculis Trochaicis unoque inſuper Iambico conſtans ; hoc modo,

véclléh ſemót bené iſráel
hábaím miẓráimah
et jáуkob íľ ubéto báu :

contra canonem VII Metricæ Hebrææ. Hoccine ut in ſe flagitium
admiſerit cultiſſimus Vates in ipſo operis limine ? Credat qui volet,
hoc à Moſe profectum.   In veros auctores culpa omnis recidat :
ſcribas, dico, male feriatos, aut etiam dormitantes, qui poſt *jaуkob*
omiſerunt vocem appoſitiſſimam אבי׳הם ; ita enim in ſuo exemplari procul dubio ſcriptum legerunt LXX Interpretes, qui ha-
bent ἅμα Ιακωϐ τῳ πατρι αυλων : ita etiam legimus in locis ſimili-
bus; אבי׳הם דן, Joſ. xix. 47. Jud. xviii, 29. אפרים אבי׳הם
1 Chron. vii. 22. ubi poſt nomen patris ſolemniter exprimitur
paternitatis relatio, quanquam alias ex iis ipſis locis notiſſima, nec
ullo modo neceſſaria.   Sic tota periodus quatuor Trochaicis le-
gitimis, iiſque bene concinnis, conſtabit : ſimulque ope Metrices,
adſtipulante Græca verſione, lociſque parallelis, loco depravato
ſua integritas reſtituitur.

5. Codex

ספר שמות

פרק א

1. ואלה שמות בני ישראל
הבאים מצרימה
את יעקב . . .
איש וביתו באו:

2. ראובן שמעון לוי ויהודה:
3. יששכר זבולן ובנימן:
4. דן ונפתלי גד ואשר:

. . . .

5. Codex Hebræus habet ויהודה, & fimiliter in verficulo
fequente ובנימן; nomen nempe utrumque cum copula. Quod
quanquam à metrica ratione non fit omnino alienum; quippe cum
nihilominus eædem ipfæ voces levi opera, mutatis et inverfis accentibus, ita notari poffint, ut ex bonis Iambicis non mali fiant
Trochaici; tamen cum, ut bene notat Harius, Trochaici rarius
occurrant, & jam præcefferit integra Periodus quatuor Trochai-
corum, vifum eft auctoritatem LXX Intt. fequi, qui neutro in
loco copulam ו agnofcunt, & Iambos ejectos poftliminio reftituere.
Hoc melius, et ex ipfa numerorum varietate concinnius, fi quid
fapiunt meæ auriculæ; quibus magiftris ac ducibus in metrica
Hebræa antiqua inftauranda præcipue utor. Verum fingulis no-
minibus in utroque verficulo copulam præponit Codex Samarita-
nus: quod perinde eft; nam iterum, mutatis accentibus, in tres
Trochaicos nullo negotio converti poffunt; hoc modo:

reúben, vefimyón, velévi,
víhudáh, vifáfcar,
vézebúlun, úbinjámin.

8. Ecce vero iterum fupinam Librariorum negligentiam!
Homines fomnolenti, ac plane vecordes: qui hunc verficulum de
propria fede deturbando, atque in alienam invehendo, et rerum
ordinem et metrum miris modis peffumdederunt. Quid enim,
quæfo? Familiae Jacobi numerum recenfet fcriptor Poetico-Hi-
toricus:

vibí col népeľ jóʑɛ jérec jáʋkob
10. ḃámiſáh veʎibʋim nápeľ.

. . . .

vajámat jófep vécol éȟaiv,
vé col hádor háhu.

úbené iʎráel páru ;
váiʎreʑu, vajírbu :

15. vajáʋaʑmu beméod méod,
vatímallé haáreʑ ótam.

vajákam mélec ȟádaľ ʋál miʑráim,
ïeló jadáʋ et jófep.

toricus : filios numerat undecim, qui cum patre fuo in Ægyptum
migraverunt; quonam igitur in loco, nifi in hoc, mentionem porro
faceret duodecimi, qui jam antea fuiffet in Ægypto? Nonne ex-
pectaret lector Hebræus numeri illius duodenarii, inter ipfos tan-
topere celebrati, completionem αμιςως atque ante omnia facien-
dam ? Ne itaque folemnis Patriarcharum Catalogus imperfectus
ac plane μειουρος evaderet, erat hic fubinjicienda Jofephi mentio.
Putafne item vatem noftrum in metrica Hebræa adeo fuiffe rudem
et indoctum, ut verfus Iambicos et Trochaicos infcite mifceret :
duos poneret Iambicos, tum unicum Trochaicum ; duos iterum
Iambicos, et unicum Trochaicum ? cujus ordinis exemplum fruftra
requires, cum nullam ejus fecerit mentionem magnus hujufce
artis jamdudum deperditæ inftaurator et ϝομοθθίης Harius ! Apage
a vate omnium μασικωτατω iftiufmodi dedecus ! Scribarum ifthæc
funt facinora. Reduc in priftinam fedem tertium membrum
commatis quinti, et fubjunge commati quarto; jam fana et
fincera, lucida et bene ordinata, concinna et numerofa, erunt
omnia. Habes Periodum primam quatuor Trochaicis verficulis
conftantem ; fecundam, quatuor Iambicis ; tertiam porro, ut mox
oftendam, Iambicis et Trochaicis duobus alternantibus. Tranf-
pofitioni autem iftius membri adftipulatur verfio LXX feniorum,
hunc ordinem, autographo Mofis haud dubie confonum, ut ex
Metro potiffimum liquet, manifefte præ fe ferens.
    Vide autem quam fcite ac belle hanc fecundam Periodum
interpunxerunt Maforetæ illi, criticorum, fi diis placet, Cory-
phæi!

‏5. וַיְהִי כָּל נֶפֶשׁ יֹצְאֵי יֶרֶךְ יַעֲקֹב
‏שִׁבְעִים נָפֶשׁ . . . .
‏וְיוֹסֵף הָיָה בְמִצְרָיִם:
‏6. וַיָּמָת יוֹסֵף וְכָל אֶחָיו
‏וְכֹל הַדּוֹר הַהוּא:

‏7. וּבְנֵי יִשְׂרָאֵל פָּרוּ
‏וַיִּשְׁרְצוּ וַיִּרְבּוּ

‏וַיַּעַצְמוּ בִּמְאֹד מְאֹד
‏וַתִּמָּלֵא הָאָרֶץ אֹתָם:

‏8. וַיָּקָם מֶלֶךְ חָדָשׁ עַל מִצְרָיִם
‏אֲשֶׁר לֹא יָדַע אֶת יוֹסֵף:

phæi! Tricolon, quod uno membro avulfo ex Tetracolo fcribæ confecerant, in tria Monocola, monftrum in Hebræa Poefi inauditum, per totidem *foph-pafukim* difcindentes. Amove, fodes, ac furcillis ejice importunas iftas interpunctiones; et membra infcite disjuncta in unam Periodum recollige. Suadet hoc, cum fententiæ et conftructionis ratio, tum Metrorum inter fe congruentia et æqualitas.

10. Quantas turbas inter Commentatores et Criticos excitaverit hic locus cum Act. vii. 14. collatus, quantumque æftuaverint in Propheta et Evangelifta in concordiam reducendis, nemo eft paulo in his literis verfatior, qui nefciat. Adi modo Wolfii Curas Philologicas in Acta Apoftolorum loco citato, qui plerorumque fententias diffentientes recenfet; quibus auditis, dices fortaffe cum Comico illo fene: "feciftis probe: incertior fum multo, quam dudum." Multi in Codd. Novi Teftamenti, quafi hoc in loco depravatos, culpam rejiciunt: ubi pro πασι legi volunt πανιας; ita Bertramus, Beza, Glaffius; vel πανιως, Jac. Cappellus: intoleranda audacia, contra conftantem omnium MSS fidem et confenfum. Ego unius Metrices ope evincam, Lucæ locum fanum effe, itemque hoc in loco LXX Intt. Verfionem, quæ cum Luca confentit; Mofis ipfius textum in mendo cubare: quod nunquam fufpicati funt Critici, craffa et pudenda metri Hebræi ignorantia præpediti. Vide enim, ut nunc fe habet lectio Hebræi Codicis, quantopere laboret metrum:

 vihí col nepeſ jóʒⱥ jérec jáykob
 . . . . . ſibⱥyim napeſ:

‏הנה

vájomér el *y*ámmo ;
20. hinneh *y*ám bené ifráel
rab vé*y*azúm mimménnu ;
habáh *na*, níthacmáh lo.

pén jirbéh, vehájah cí tikrén*u*
mílhamáh, venófap gám hu
25. *y*al fón*ε*nu, venílham banu,
ve*y*álah mín haárez.

vájafímu *y*álaiv fár*ε* míffim,
lémay*án *y*anóto béfiblótam :
vajíben *y*ár*ε* mifcenót lepár*y*oh,
30. et pítom, v'ét ra*y*ámfes.

tum amoto ac tranfpofito altero illo membro, quod fuperiori Periodo
fubjiciendum modo demonftravi, fequitur,

vejámat jófep vécol éhaiv,
vécol hádor háhu.

Sentis nimirum unam alteramque voculam e fecundo verficulo ex-
cidiffe, quæ ad fupplendum verfum Trochaicum, verficulo al-
terno fequenti refpondentem, defiderantur : ipfas nimirum voces,
quas LXX Intt. et Lucas in fuo exemplari legerunt,

ħámifáh *ve*ħibyim nápeħ.

πεντε και ἑϐδομηκοντα, LXX. ἑϐδομηκοντα και πεντε, Lucas. Nota
autem vocem שׁפֶֿנ, pro perfona, mafculino genere fæpiufcule
venire : vid. Gen. xlvi. 22, 25. et Jer. lii. 30. Hanc autem
lectionem etiam hiftoriæ veritas poftulat. Recenfet Mofes Jacobi
familiam, quæ una cum ipfo in Ægyptum migravit. Quid vero ?
nonne uxorum filiorum familias, quotquot erant fuperftites (nam
numerus incertus eft) habenda erat ratio ? An cuiquam perfuaferis,
Mofen in ea fuiffe fententia, ut, cum barbaris quibufdam hodi-
ernis, negaret mulieres animabus effe præditas, adeoque inter
animas numerari non debuiffe ? Dices fortaffe, nurus Jacobi non
poffe cenferi in illorum numero, qui e femore Jacobi proceffe-
runt. Vah! quafi ita ad vivum refecanda effet Mofis locutio:
nurus funt filiæfamilias, adeoque familiæ pars ; atque id folum
voluit

9. וַיֹּאמֶר אֶל עַמּוֹ
הִנֵּה עַם בְּנֵי יִשְׂרָאֵל
רַב וְעָצוּם מִמֶּנּוּ:

10. הָבָה . . . נִתְחַכְּמָה לוֹ

פֶּן יִרְבֶּה וְהָיָה כִּי תִקְרֶאנָה
מִלְחָמָה וְנוֹסַף גַּם הוּא
עַל שֹׂנְאֵינוּ וְנִלְחַם בָּנוּ
וְעָלָה מִן הָאָרֶץ:

11. וַיָּשִׂימוּ עָלָיו שָׂרֵי מִסִּים
לְמַעַן עַנֹּתוֹ בְּסִבְלֹתָם
וַיִּבֶן עָרֵי מִסְכְּנוֹת לְפַרְעֹה,
אֶת פִּתֹם וְאֶת רַעַמְסֵס:

voluit Mofes. Quid? num Jacobus ipfe ex fuomet ipfius femore
prodiit? Quod ut affirmes, æquè neceffe eft; nam certum eft Jacobum in numero feptuaginta perfonarum includi, fi pro eo numero
pugnas, ejufque veram rationem inire velis. Conftat enim per-
fonas ex femore Jacobi revera egreffas, quæ cum ipfo in Ægyptum
migraverunt, fuiffe numero fexaginta fex: vide Gen. xlvi. 8—26.
adde Jofephum, duofque ejus filios, et Jacobum ipfum, numerum
habes feptuaginta. Sed Jofephus, duoque ejus filii, erant prius
in Ægypto, nec cum Jacobo in Ægyptum migraverunt; adeoque
perfonis hic annumeratis accenferi non poffunt. Itaque numero
fexaginta fex adde novem nurus; (nam Judæ uxor in Cananæa
jam ante deceffcrat, Gen. xxxviii. 12. et una præterea aliqua
reliquarum;) jam habes numerum feptuaginta quinque capitum
familiæ Jacobi, quæ cum ipfo in Ægyptum migravit. De locis
autem vatis noftri huic parallelis binis, Gen. xlvi. 27. Deut. x.
22. pofthac videro, libros iftos, in verficulos item difpofitos, et
Metrices ope integritati fuæ reftitutos, aliquando donaturus.

18. הלֹ. " Heb. alter. Quod plene quidem fcribitur; fed
" metrum poftulat, ut contractè legatur לה, ut fæpe alias." Hæc
in Pfalm i. verfic. 12.

22. Hac in Periodo alicubi laborat metrum. Repofui particulam
אֵ ת in ultimo verficulo; cujus veftigium extat in verfione LXX

5   Intt.

vecáaťér jeyánnu óto,
cen jírbeh, vécen jiproz;
vajákuzú mipné bené ifrácl :

vajáybidú mizráim
35. et béne ífraél bepárec.

vaímaráru ét ħajéhem,
báyabódah káťah :

baħómer úbilbénim,
ubécol yábodáh bafádeh,
40. veét col yábodátam,
aťér yabdú bahém bepárec.

vájomér meléc mizráim
lámejáldot háyibríjot,
ʃeťém haéħat ťíprah,
45. veťém haťénit púyah :

vajómer béjallédcen háyibríjot,
uréitén yal háobnáim,
im bén hu, váhamítten óto,
v'im bát hi, váħajétah.

Intt. Exemplar. Vat. Διυτι ΟΥΝ κατασοφισωμιθα. Eſt et alia ratio
iſthoc ulcuſculum ſanandi ; hoc modo :
  vájomér el yámmo :
  hínneh yám bení ifráel,
  hámon ráb, ve*jayazóm* mimménnu ;
  hábah nítħacmáh lo :
nimirum ſupplendo lacunas tertii verſiculi ex verſione Græca, quæ
fic habet ; μιγα πληθ⊕-, και ισχιιι ίπιρ ήμας. Sed prius placet ;
ut minus recedens à textu Hebræo.

23. Tikren:u

‏12. וכאשר יענו אתו
כן ירבה וכן יפרץ
ויקצו מפני בני ישראל :

‏13. ויעבדו מצרים
את בני ישראל בפרך :

‏14. וימררו את חייהם
בעבדה קשה

בחמר ובלבנים
ובכל עבדה בשדה
. את כל עבדתם
אשר עבדו בהם בפרך :

‏15. ויאמר מלך מצרים
למילדת העברית
אשר שם האחת שפרה
ושם השנית פועה :

‏16. ויאמר בילדכן את העבריות
וראיתן על האבנים
אם בן הוא והמתן אתו
ואם בת הוא וחיה :

23. Tikrenu. Ita omnino legendum, cum Cod. Sam. LXX. Intt. et aliis compluribus veterum. Quod ad metrum attinet, nihil interest.

28. " Hebr. *limayan*, inquit Harius; sed disyllabum esse " ubicunque occurrit, omnia exempla monstrant." Not. in Psalm. v. 18. Verum, quod pace tanti auctoris dixerim, hoc in loco est evidens exemplum in contrariam partem.

40. *veeth*. Ita MS. Erfurt. 3. (vide Bib. Heb. Michaelis) proculdubio recte: deest enim syllaba ad explendum versiculum.

46. Heb.

50. vatírená haméjaldót et háelóhim,
veló yafú caáľer díbber
élehén meléc mizráim,
váteħájená et hájeladim.

vajíkra *páryoh* lámejáldot,
55. vajómer láhen, máduy
yáfitén hadábar házeh,
váteħájená et hájeládim.

vátomárna hámejáldot
él pharyóh, ci ló canáſhim
60. hámizríjot háyibríjot,
cí ħajót henáh, beťérem tábo
élehén haméjalédet véjaládu.

vájeťéb elóhim lámejáldot ;
váireb háyam, vájayázmu méod.

---

46. Heb. *et* hayibríjot : fed omittenda eft, metri gratia, par-
ticula *et* ; vel forfan, quod magis fufpicor, vox *vajomer*, a librariis
otiofe et inutiliter repetita ab initio commatis præcedentis.

49. Vide modo, quam turpiter rurfum hallucinati funt ofci-
tantes fcribæ ; qui nobis hic exhibent *vaŝajah*, craffo errore, et
manifefto folœcifmo, pro *vaŝajetha*, quod habet Cod. Sam.
quam lectionem, haud dubie finceram, reftituimus. Metrum
quod attinet, perinde erit, feu in eodem verficulo *v'im* legamus
μετοσυλλαβικως, feu *yale* verficulo fecundo; ut hujus periodi fecundus
et quartus fint Trochaici. Prius prætulimus ; quoniam ne lit-
terulam quidem in Textu facile mutamus fine codicum vel ver-
fionum antiquarum auctoritate, una vocula excepta, fe pro aľer.

54. Pro *paryoh* hoc in loco textus Hebræus habet *melec mizraim* ;
incuria librariorum, qui e duabus locutionibus fynonymis aliquo-
ties recurrentibus unam pro altera, uti fit, pofuerunt. Quorum
errorem palam facit vel ipfe contextus : nam poftquam dixiffet
Mofes, " Et accerfivit PHARAO obftetrices;'' addit, planè con-
grue ad priorem loquendi formam, " Et refponderunt obſtetrices
PHARAONI."

17. וַתִּירֶאןָ הַמְיַלְדֹת אֶת הָאֱלֹהִים
וְלֹא עָשׂוּ כַּאֲשֶׁר דִּבֶּר
אֲלֵיהֶן מֶלֶךְ מִצְרָיִם
וַתְּחַיֶּיןָ אֶת הַיְלָדִים:

18. וַיִּקְרָא מֶלֶךְ מִצְרַיִם לַמְיַלְּדֹת
וַיֹּאמֶר לָהֶן מַדּוּעַ
עֲשִׂיתֶן הַדָּבָר הַזֶּה
וַתְּחַיֶּיןָ אֶת הַיְלָדִים:

19. וַתֹּאמַרְןָ הַמְיַלְּדֹת
אֶל פַּרְעֹה כִּי לֹא כַנָּשִׁים
הַמִּצְרִיֹּת הָעִבְרִיֹּת
כִּי חָיוֹת הֵנָּה בְּטֶרֶם תָּבוֹא
אֲלֵהֶן הַמְיַלֶּדֶת וְיָלָדוּ:

20. וַיֵּיטֶב אֱלֹהִים לַמְיַלְּדֹת
וַיִּרֶב הָעָם וַיַּעַצְמוּ מְאֹד:

PHARAONI." Sed et lectionem *paryoh* prorfus effIagitat metrum ;
quippe quod aliter recto talo ftare omnino non poteft. Atque
hanc infignem emendationem, à Metro depoftulatam, plane con-
firmat Cod. Sam.

68. En verficulum in textu Hebræo & fenfu & metro pariter
mancum et imperfectum! Inducitur Pharao fuis mandata edens,
hoc modo : " Mafculum omnem, quicunque natus fuerit, in
" fluvium projicite." Papæ! quid audio? quid fibi vult Rex
Ægyptius? num ut mafculos infantes omnes, fuos etiam una
cum Hebræis, nullo difcrimine, mitterent illico in profluentem?
Egregium vero ποιημα λαων! hominem, feu potius belluam, ve-
cordem atque immanem! Tu vero, fi me audis, in librarios
ftupidos et fomnilentos omnem culpam rejicito. Nos fi vocem,
quam ifti fupina negligentia prætermiferunt, in fedem fuam poftliminio revocamus, ecquid erit pretii? Eccam ipfam prorfus :
לַעֲבָרִים!

col háben hájillód *l-yibrim.*

Qram,

65. vájehí, ci járeu hámejáldot
   ét haélohím, vajáyaſláhcm báttim.

vajézav páryoh lécol yámmo lémor,
col háben, hájillód *leyíbrim*,
hajórah táſlicúhu,
70. vecól habát teħájun.

Quam, quod fanĉte adſeverare poſſum, Metrum ipſum primitus ſuggeſſit ; tum ſenſus, Cod. Sam. LXX. Intt. firmaverunt. I nunc, et nega Metricen Hebræam in vera Codicis Hcbræi leĉtione inſtauranda quicquam proficere !

Sed hæc haĉtenus, in primum ſolummodo Exodi Caput: quæ nos levi opera, et planè αυτοσχιδιως, in chartam conjecimus ; non eum locum ideo ſeligentes, quod in eo plura, quam in alio fere
quovis

‏‎21. וַיְהִי כִּי יָרְאוּ הַמְיַלְּדֹת
אֶת הָאֱלֹהִים וַיַּעַשׂ לָהֶם בָּתִּים:

‏‎22. וַיְצַו פַּרְעֹה לְכָל עַמּוֹ לֵאמֹר
כָּל הַבֵּן הַיִּלּוֹד . . .
הַיְאֹרָה תַּשְׁלִיכֻהוּ
וְכָל הַבַּת תְּחַיּוּן:

quovis Pentateuchi capite, ope Metrices reſtituere nos et emendare poſſe confideremus; ſed fortuito incidentes, periculi tantum et ſpeciminis cauſa. Tu autem, Lector, his laboris noſtri primitiis utere, fruere; ſed totum hoc, quantumcunque eſt, præclaro Harii reperto acceptum refer, et Genio Metrices Hebrææ inſtauratori, ſuſpitatori, ſtatori, hecatomben litato.

I have

I have now purfued this fubject as far as I
intended; much further perhaps than it will
be thought neceffary for me to have done.
And, I think, I have fhewn, what the Hebrew
Metre is not; namely, that it is not Bifhop
Hare's Metre. But I cannot venture to proceed upon that axiom, on which you, Sir, fo
very much infift; and to conclude, that,
" from ' knowing, negatively, what it is not,
" we may with great certainty collect, po-
" fitively, what it is." On the contrary, I
find, I muft be fatisfied with much lefs fan-
guine pretenfions, and content myfelf with
joining in the humble wifh of Cicero: " Uti-
" nam tam facile poffem vera invenire, quam
" falfa convincere!"

You may poffibly tell me again, that, inftead of confuting the Bifhop's fyftem, I have
made a joke of it, and turned it to ridicule.
All the apology which I fhall offer upon this
occafion, if any be thought needful, is this:
that if an object, by being placed in a proper,
a juft, and a true light, appears ridiculous;
he who fo placeth it, is not to be blamed; the
fault is not in him, but in the object itfelf.

One word more, Sir, and I have done. It
may be expected, that I fhould give fome
reafon, why I do not anfwer your Latin Epiftle
in the fame language. The plain truth of

' EDWARDS Preliminary Differtation, p. 18. Prolegom.
in Libb. Poeticos, p. 32.

the

the matter is this : as foon as I had read and
confidered your Epiftle, I fat down to write
to you my thoughts more at large upon the
fubject, merely for your private perufal, with
no defign of making them public ; being
very unwilling to try the patience of my
readers any more upon fo dry, fo unfruitful,
and fo unedifying an argument. When I had
written about half of what you now fee,
finding it run to fuch a length, and fo far
ftill from drawing to a conclufion, I threw
it afide with difguft and indignation ; and determined never to trouble myfelf any more,
or you at all, with it. Almoft a year afterwards I happened to light upon my papers :
I looked them over, having then quite for-
gotten the particular contents of them ; and
finding what I had written to be clear, as I
thought, and conclufive, I was induced to
refume my defign ; but could not per-
fuade myfelf to take the trouble of altering
the form of it : and I imagined, that it
might poffibly be of further ufe than I at
firft propofed. When an Hypothefis comes
ftrongly recommended under the fanction of
a great name ; when it is confidently appealed
to as firmly and unqueftionably eftabiifhed,
and urged as fufficient warrant for intro-
ducing, or even confirming, emendations and
alterations of the Hebrew Text of the Holy
Scriptures ; the matter, however infignificant

in itself, becomes of real importance in its confequences, and merits ferious attention, and a ftrict examination. And when men of learning and genius mifapply their labours, and throw away their abilities, in the purfuit of a mere fhadow; and by their example and authority draw after them younger ftudents, capable of better things, into the fame vain purfuit; to convince them and others of the delufion they are under, is faving ufeful hands to the public, and doing a general fervice to the Common-wealth of Letters,

I am,

Reverend S I R,

Your moft humble Servant,

Nov. 20,
1765.   R. LOWTH.

E R R A T A.

P. 17. l. 27. r. attempt,
28.   16. r. *ănd hĕll*, as λἴγἔῐ̄ν.

BOOKS printed for A. MILLAR in the Strand, and J. DODSLEY in Pall-Mall.

DE Sacra Poefi Hebræorum Prælectiones Academicæ, Oxonii habitæ a Roberto Lowth, D. D.

Johannis Davidis Michaelis, Philof. Profeff. Ord. et Societatis Regiæ Scientiarum Goettingenfis Collegæ in Roberti Lowth Prælectiones de facra Poefi Hebræorum Notæ et Epimetra: ex Goettingenfi editione Prælectionum.

The Life of William of Wykeham, Bifhop of Winchefter, collected from Records, Regifters, MSS. and other authentic Evidences, by Robert Lowth, D. D.

A fhort Introduction to Englifh Grammar, with critical Notes. Two Editions, one on Writing Paper, price 3s. and the other for the Ufe of Schools, price 1s. 6d.

A Letter to the Right Reverend Author of the Divine Legation of Mofes demonftrated; in anfwer to an Appendix to the Fifth Volume of that Work: With an Appendix, containing a former Literary Correfpondence, by a late Profeffor in the Univerfity of Oxford, the 4th Edition.

www.ingramcontent.com/pod-product-compliance
Lightning Source LLC
Chambersburg PA
CBHW032352020726
47499CB00008B/2710

9783337318291